720.922 COO

Wolf D. Prix

Dynamic Forces

COOP HIMMELB(L)AU   BMW WELT Munich

Essay by Sanford Kwinter

Kristin Feireiss (ed.)

PRESTEL

MUNICH · BERLIN · LONDON · NEW YORK

Contents

Forewords

Architecture as a sign: that is the future, according to Coop Himmelb(l)au. This is why the BMW Group chose the design conceived by the architects at Coop Himmelb(l)au for BMW Welt. We wanted our high aspirations for the content of this building to be reflected in the architecture. We wanted to create a building that acts as a messenger: for the BMW brand, for our corporate culture and, not least, for the city of Munich.

BMW Welt stands as a beacon for the BMW brand. The building radiates dynamism and innovative power, the values the BMW brand stands for. Everyone who encounters the brand there — whether as visitor or customer — will enjoy a memorable experience. They will feel what it is that makes BMW so special. For our customers, BMW Welt is not only an entertainment attraction but also the delivery center for their new car. When they come to pick up their vehicle, we offer them an exceptional opportunity to experience all the facets of the BMW brand.

One of the requirements we set for Coop Himmelb(l)au was to translate the central values of our corporate culture, such as flexibility and openness, into architecture. What resulted is a structure that opens up a whole range of creative possibilities and is geared to the demands of the future. BMW Welt is a place of encounter in which we convey visions and innovations, and where people will be inspired by the products of BMW. It is intended to function as a communication platform that both emanates and assimilates new impulses.

Another important goal of BMW Welt was to lend another groundbreaking architectural accent to our Munich location. The building adds a further chapter to the series made up of the BMW Tower, the so-called Four Cylinders, built in 1973, and the BMW Museum completed the same year. With the bold cylindrical form taken by its company headquarters, designed by Viennese architect Karl Schwanzer, the BMW Group already began to set architectural standards three decades ago.

When we awarded the contract for BMW Welt to Coop Himmelb(l)au, we knew full well that theirs was a courageous design. 34 years after Schwanzer's Four Cylinders, his student, Professor Wolf Prix, has realized with his "floating roof landscape" for BMW Welt architecture that is acknowledged by experts as venturing to the limits of what is feasible today.

With BMW Welt, the BMW Group has set yet another benchmark of urban planning, a must-see for all visitors to the Bavarian capital interested in architecture and technology as well as design and innovation. I extend a cordial welcome to all those who would like to experience the BMW brand in these fascinating surroundings!

Ernst Baumann
Member of the Board of BMW AG

The plan was to publish a book about BMW Welt by Coop Himmel-b(l)au, covering everything from winning the competition to the completion of the building: a formidable task given the complexity of this mega-project. What ultimately resulted goes far beyond this initial objective. In view of the extraordinary cultural and spatial dimensions of what is a unique building in recent architectural history, the entire theoretical and architectural scope of the œuvre of Wolf D. Prix unfolds here, with analogies drawn to earlier works and an intensification of his theoretical insights. What becomes evident in the process is the breathtaking consistency, verging on an uncompromising vigor that does not shy away from confrontation, with which Prix has remained true to the convictions on architecture and society that he acquired early on — all the while determined, despite setbacks, to realize them in his architecture. BMW Welt is an impressive example of this steadfastness.

As a Viennese architectural revolutionary who does not deny that he, along with every other intellectual in this city on the Danube, cannot escape the sway of Freud, Wolf D. Prix has remained committed over the course of four decades to achieving the kind of architecture that can make a contribution to the development of society. BMW Welt, which for the first time offered Prix an opportunity to formulate what he calls a hybrid building, mirrors this attitude.

A further thread running through his entire oeuvre, as through this project, is the attempt to come to terms with dynamic forces as a form-giving element and to translate this energy into architecture on a grand scale. This grand scale is certainly on view in the case of BMW Welt. It was then a small but logical step to give this book the title "Dynamic Forces."

One thing is clear: if it is to do justice to the building and its architect, this first publication on BMW Welt must work on several different levels. One level is, as already mentioned, the key role played by this building within the overall oeuvre of Coop Himmelb(l)au. Another level is the design and construction process, which is presented by way of a dialogue between technical explanations that are specialized but always highly interesting and informative, and detailed photos of the various building phases, which provide fascinating last-chance views of the hidden world behind the now-finished facades of this complex construction.

Both texts and photos are indispensable for an understanding of this gigantic structure and its lightweight yet powerful presence. In deciding to place considerable emphasis in this book on the construction phases, a great deal of persuasion was needed on the part of the editor, since for the architect these are merely steps on the way toward the actual goal: the finished building. And the magical appeal of this building is sure to fascinate the observer, thanks to the many pages of photo spreads of the completed BMW Welt at the beginning and end of the book, the work of outstanding photographers including Hélène Binet, Ari Marcopoulos and Gerald Zugmann.

Kristin Feireiss

Sanford Kwinter
Architecture and Combustion

To this observer, accustomed to spending months of every year where the great cyclonic pressure systems of the central American plain intersect those of the Gulf Coast, Coop Himmelb(l)au's BMW Welt transcends any image the mind can present to itself of an object building, of a *thing* assembled of plans and parts and reasons. It presents rather a phenomenon less distinct and more primordial, provoking almost primitive terror like the traveling "acts of god" or *forces majeures* (as insurance practice calls them) that reshape landscapes, topple buildings, take lives — a thing beyond human control, product of forces and causes that suspend concepts while inspiring trembling, awe, and the dim awakenings of supernatural explanation. We are instantly reminded that *weather*, and not only sea, possesses a scope that subjugates the senses and understanding; either way, the experience of both lies at the foundations of the famous "dynamic sublime" that marked the far boundary of Kant's Aesthetics. The dynamic sublime enters the human picture, Kant tells us, at the precarious point where the reassurances of form give way to formlessness — the surging ocean in Kant's famous example — producing an encounter that allows the mind to experience parts of reality as fearsome without actually needing to be afraid of them.

It can be said that architecture has always sought to achieve this precise ideal, chasing it perennially on the side of beauty (through "satisfaction in quality") or mathematics (through ideas or within the abstract plasticity of thought). The dynamic sublime however belongs to a different, far less accessible order, to that which is both concrete yet boundless at the same time and therefore connected to a "satisfaction of quantity" that surpasses us yet whose infinity we can experience intimately even without comprehending. We encounter it typically only through a provocation of Nature; and by the

act of incorporating into the imagination our relationship to the irresistible and overwhelming forces that compose it (what it would do to us) "the mind can make felt the proper sublimity of its [own] destination." It is rare for the literary arts to attempt such an approximation — Musil's *Man Without Qualities* or Broch's *Death of Virgil* might be two hubristic exceptions: more likely music (Wagner?) or even film (Tarkovski?) may have approached it. But architecture stands alone among the spatial arts in staking a claim to the sublime although its efforts have generally fallen short, becoming trapped either in form or in reason. In the work of Coop Himmelb(l)au, and perhaps only now thanks to the scale of work achieved in BMW Welt, has the dynamic sublime been achieved, shall we say, in a human work. Hovering on Munich's horizon like a great warping storm of unknowable power and duration, and suspended perversely between the tensioned tents of Frei Otto's canonical Olympic Stadium and the precision-machined pistons and inverted cupola of Karl Schwanzer's BMW Corporate Headquarters, one's first apprehension of the new BMW Welt, with its uncanny vortical compression at its south end and vast, trailing stratus-cloud-like release, cannot help but startle even as it titillates. For *weather* is in fact nothing more than pneumatic *sea*, and here architecture is for the first time an inseparable part of it, realizing a three-decade-long preparation by the Coop-Himmelb(l)au project to make architecture present itself to experience at once as cloud, panther and flame.[1]

The ambition to create and emit clouds is unique to Coop Himmelb(l)au. Over the decades they have spoken repeatedly of breaching whales to evoke both the paradox and the necessity of vast things — of mass in general — to emancipate itself from the rectilinear — and bourgeois — world of gravity. They were the first

Hard Space, Vienna, Austria, 1970

to see architecture as a volatile substance not only capable of burning but of *realizing itself* in the process of combustion. It was one of the great conundrums of 18th-century chemistry that many burned, oxidized, or "dephlogisticated" substances would actually gain weight when undergoing these transformations rather than lose it. It was long suggested that burning represented a release of "airs" that were essentially buoyant and whose departure from the original substance left it more "grave" than before. Either way, one was already beginning to suspect, and was soon after able to prove, that fire and life were powerfully and mysteriously connected. Antoine Lavoisier showed not only that biological respiration was actually a form of combustion, but that both involved a transfer and transformation of "airs". At that time one still believed in some kind of "immaterial" that was called phlogiston; it was responsible for fire, it made things light, released heat and gave character to different types of "air". Phlogiston was not so much a thing in the end but a set of demonstrable and interesting properties unified under a single heading. It described the volatility, transformability and levity of life in contradistinction to the inertia and stasis of what does not and cannot burn. And for Coop Himmelb(l)au one thing mattered above all, that architecture should *blaze*.[2]

The search for volatility within the inert became a political and an almost moral quest. In this sense they are the indisputable godparents of the widespread search among young architects today for a materialist-vitalist foundation for thinking about form and process.[3] The Coop Himmelb(l)au project was in fact never precisely a *de*-constructivist one at all; it was an attempt to volatilize architecture and life through the concoction of mixtures — by combining architecture with whatever could induce it to combust, to move, to unfold,

to escape the complacent confines of *place*. And this finally is the true meaning of their famous slogan: *"There is no ground plan!"* Architecture rather is an unfolding, an exfoliation of the social and other phlogistons trapped uniformly throughout bourgeois matter. Space is not determined by a privileged and pre-given plane but by the infinity of potential expansions that can be ignited at any and every point whatever. No better example of this principle exists than in Coop Himmelb(l)au's early methods of drawing (Formfindung) that are often and wrongly associated with random or automatic surrealist technique. On the contrary, their drawing techniques are examples of what one could call their "corrosive"[4] method of invention, their means of developing one form out of another by applying an external force or agent that causes it to *react*. In several works of the early 1980s blind pencil scribbles were produced to be subsequently harvested for lucid structure. The so-called reading of the drawing was actually a burning, an adding (of a gas), *a combustion* of the information embedded in it, a development through reaction, an incorporation of external forces (the production of an "oxide"), or to put it another way, an expenditure and a volatilization of the drawing's "chemical" potential. It was, as the 18th century might have said, the systematic release of imprisoned phlogiston — a setting ablaze. No wonder they dreamed of everything that escapes and floats, obsessed about flames and wings and relentlessly produced lofted, levitated and flickering structures.[5]

In this, their work recalls and rejoins that of another 18th-century project, at once contemporary with Lavoisier's and Dalton's[6] and fully part of the history of "airs" that lies at the foundation of our technical and scientific modernity, that of the Montgolfier Brothers in France who developed the first buoyant megastructures by har-

House with the flying roof, London, GB, 1973

nessing the levity of certain types of air for their navigational balloons. Joseph Montgolfier, like Prix and Swiczinsky, was obsessed
with clouds and noted one day how laundry drying over a fire would
billow and form pockets of air that rose upward. Observing further
how burning paper and other substances would be sent airborne
for certain distances by unknown forces, the brothers (Joseph and
Etienne) set about building a structure of enormous scale to demonstrate the lifting capacity of *Montgolfier air* (it was initially believed
that combustion produced an air of specific quality and levity, and
only later was it understood that temperature alone raised normal
air's volume and lowered its weight relative to ambient air). Their co-
lossal tafetta balloons and the airships to which they later gave rise,
stand at the technical and tectonic origin of the Coop Himmelb(l)au
project and of the revolutionary BMW Welt. For only in this chemico-
tectonic tradition do immensity and levity go hand in hand.

As in so many recent Coop Himmelb(l)au projects, the images of
chrysalis (or crystal) and cloud are paired together in the BMW Welt
cosmos. The extraordinarily ornate filigree of the cyclonic vortex that
both anchors and uproots the building like a spasm of expanding
plasma is an almost insectile structure seemingly generated by the
type of cooperative approximations made possible only by colonies
of interacting agents. The radical regularity and anisotropy of the
structure together make it impossible to tell whether it is expanding
or contracting; all that is certain is that it is in continual formation,
saturated with forces in perpetual management of their mixtures,
durations and directions. It is, more than anything else, a dynamo
of structure and impetus that is being directed outward in continual
modulation, like structural weather, a product of pneumatic and re-
ticular behaviors and relationships that are not bounded in either

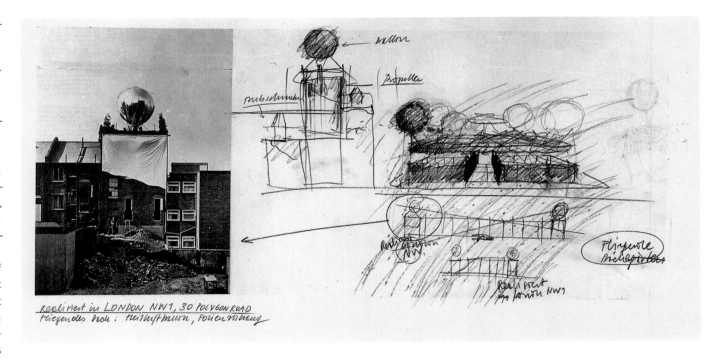

Large Cloud Scene — Super Sommer, Vienna, Austria, 1976
Blazing Wing, Graz, Austria, 1980

space or time. Just as the proverbial butterfly in the Amazon is said to generate hurricanes in distant Indonesia, one notes here just as there that it is precisely the unbroken tissue of causality with its indifference to scale that characterizes the new plane of reality in which problems of matter and structure are today being worked out. The butterfly floats (Mohammed Ali) as does the cloud, but it disturbs air and sends it moving into the algorithmically determined atmosphere like a micro-architectural intervention seeking its eventual point of combustion or catastrophe; its wings a product and mirror-remnant of their chrysalidic origin, perfect transitory architectures that punctuate an always transforming and centerless lifecycle[7]. Even in time (and indeed especially so) *there is no ground plan!* In the secret history of matter, there is only weather.

Out of the crystal-vortex and extending northward blooms the great cloud like a huge bladder maintained aloft by air pressure differentials or other mysteries of aviation or chemistry. Here and there the desperate mind that resists magical explanation scans the void's interior in search of telltale supportive structure. Only after a certain time does one spy two fine, camouflaged, and uncannily fragile tapered columns, angling their way to the perforated metallic ceiling that lofts overhead. These are the only signs — and they are barely credible — that one is still on planet earth, subject to the physics of inertia in its specific atmosphere and gravitational field. The interior void is otherwise of a scale seen only in modern stadiums, yet the drama that anchors it is not the rational field of rules and distributions that determine a game, but once again a geometrical figure of expansion and continuity in the form of two winding gyres of track, one of which — the major pedestrian one — stores energy visibly within itself as it twists and deflects off every

one of its axes before springing from its orbit entirely to project off the site through an opening in the upper membrane wall and across the Lerchenauer Strasse. This is an architectural performance now on a fully infrastructural scale, almost a civic work like a disconnected bridge (or one that simply bridges between 4th-dimensional realities?) or a deliberately perverted road system that applies an Einstein-Podolsky-Rosen[8] equation to the rationalist *Autobahnen* to which it is ultimately connected. Along the more minor of these spiroform ramps (which renders the Corbusian promenade a hopeless archaism) automobiles pass as they are ceremoniously turned over to their new owners. The calculus of the curves here is naturally a product of performance envelopes and machine tolerances (*Arbeit* at slow speed) suggesting an architecture partly of *internal combustion*, or at least one embedded within the hidden determinacies that are a legacy of the century of the chemical engine. Let no one be fooled by the egregious watch-like refinement of every fitting, joint and connection in BMW Welt: this is the space partly of Mad Max and his ilk as well.[9] Indeed nothing comes more immediately to mind than the erotic/thanatic "overpass fantasies" of J. G. Ballard's novel *Crash*, or the peculiarly Texan orgies of indoor oil-consumption such as the demolition derbies that for decades took place under the rotunda of Houston's epochal Astrodome[10] room.

In approaching the dynamic sublime, BMW Welt transcends almost all of the criteria that have customarily been associated with architecture — fixity, stability, finitude — and approximates the indeterminate, unbounded and labile aspects of an unruly and unpredictable Nature. At the heart of the Coop Himmelb(l)au project there lies not a simplistic antagonism to gravity but an alchemical im-

Blazing Wing
Pencil and cigarette-lighter, 1980

pulse to transform matter, to invest it with social agency above all, to revolutionize it and in so doing to revolutionize the human world that makes it and is made by it. The original image of abundance and freedom was the flame. The flame emblematized an architecture set loose from the rigidities and determinacies of solids and grids. The flame is a mixture of gases in a still shapeless state of excitation and action. As a guiding image and ethos, it soon gave way to pneumatic accumulations of increasingly refined and relaxed orders — drifting clouds for example, or expanding vortexes and crystals. These represented a new class of forms that effectively and indisputably emancipated architecture from the social and cognitive tyrannies of the ground plan forever after.[11] But behind both these images there lies the mysterious and silent action of another figure, the one that accounts for the predominantly social and urbanist preoccupation of the Coop Himmelb(l)au enterprise, the image of a solitary hunting animal so embedded in its ecology and context that it is almost never seen, the jungle panther. For those who track them, the panther (jaguar, leopard, cougar, tiger) is the most elusive of animals, so hard to observe that they are often equated with the breath and density of the jungle itself.[12] Their style of movement and appearance is the stuff of legend: a sudden irruption of horrific combusting power, an explosion on the order of a biological big bang. The panther is always the top predator in its food chain, compressing within itself a greater extent of the "caloric" territory in which it lives than any other form. Less an animal than a thermodynamic cycle, the panther is an explosive dilation that alternates with a contraction that concentrates a great sum of matter and energy within itself. It is the violent pulse of all other life, it is what makes the jungle and the jungle is what makes it. Yet the panther is an

animal of guile and grace, unmatched in the elegance and efficiency of its movements and habit. The panther is at once the volatility of the flame and the immanence of the cloud. But beyond this it is also the ecstasy of matter in eternal erotic combustion. The philosopher-economist Georges Bataille once wrote, "the sex act is to time what the tiger is to space", presumably to remind us that life is an infinite orgy of matter, a quest to discover the ways in which matter and energy can be combined to create sensation and action and not only bankable form. In architecture the work of Coop Himmelb(l)au may be alone in exploring the performances of forms and not only their consolidations. In BMW Welt we have perhaps the first appearance in architecture of the panther's fatal, ecstatic and infinitely renewable lunge.[13]

1 Cf. "Coop Himmelb(l)au Is Not a Color" (1968), "The Cloud" (1968), "Architecture Must Blaze" (1980), "Architecture is Now" (1982), "The Architecture of Clouds" (1995), in: *Get Off of My Cloud: Wolf D. Prix Coop Himmelb(l)au Texts 1968–2005*, Hatje Cantz 2005

2 "Architecture Must Blaze" Ibid.

3 The "bible" for this quest is Reiser and Umemoto's *Atlas of Novel Tectonics*, Princeton Architectural Press, New York 2006.

4 Corrosion, combustion and respiration had in common the fact that they required and fixed oxygen — thus "Oxys" (acid) + "gen" (generating) according to Lavoisier's original formulation. Lavoisier disproved the phlogiston theory by showing that oxygen is what burns in a conflagration. He believed that all acids contained this special type of "air" that he called oxygen.

5 "Wing of Fire/Blazing Wing: Architecture Must Blaze" (Graz, 1980), "Project for Supersommer" (Vienna 1976), "Hot Flat" (project, 1978), "The Temperature Wing" (project, 1980), "Red Angel" (Vienna, 1981).

6 On Dalton's role as Lavoisier's English nemesis and interlocutor see Poirier, Bensaude-Vincent and Stengers, and Guerlac in footnote 13.

7 In our methodological example, the drawing plays the role of Chrysalis or seed, the Cloud is its expansion (ex-plosion) or unfolding. In BMW Welt this narrative of genesis is acted out formally and syntactically.

8 The EPR hypothesis is among the most famous of Einstein's *Gedankenexperimente* (1935). Its purpose was to undermine quantum physical theory by pushing its principles to illogical conclusions. Among these was the principle of entanglement in which two particles remain formally linked to one another even when separated by enormous distances. The other was that an operation performed on one could be transmitted to the other instantaneously, regardless of the usual constraints of time and space. Bizarrely, the EPR hypothesis has received considerable experimental confirmation since it was first invented.

9 *Mad Max* (1979), Dir. George Miller. Apocalyptic Australian science fiction film in which global oil shortages give way to a total breakdown of social order and result in a highway frontier-world of bike gangs, motor violence and vigilante highway patrols.

10 The Houston Astrodome (1966), dubbed by its conceiver the "Eighth Wonder of the World", was the first sports arena to have a roof over its entire playing field. It was specifically designed so that there would not be a single column to obstruct either the players' or the spectators' view.

11 A revolution that Frank Gehry, for example, never achieved. Gehry's works conserve, almost with a vengeance, the most attenuated and routinized plans, like cryptic remnants of the regressive social organizations and institutions they serve. In the plan everything is either conserved or blown apart. Nothing revolutionary ever happened outside of the plan. The projects of Coop Himmelb(l)au and Frank Gehry are thus diametrically opposed.

12 Whence the famous rhetorical device of "becoming invisible" that drove the famous British comedic television series *The Pink Panther*.

13 Immanuel Kant, *Critique of Aesthetic Judgment*, Oxford University Press, Oxford and New York 1952; Jean-Pierre Poirier, *Lavoisier: Chemist, Biologist, Economist*, University of Pennsylvania Press, Philadelphia 1993; Bernadette Bensaude-Vincent and Isabelle Stengers, *A History of Chemistry*, Harvard University Press, Cambridge 1996; Henry Guerlac, *Antoine-Laurent Lavoisier: Chemist and Revolutionary*, Scribners, New York 1975 and *Lavoisier, The Crucial Year: The Background and Origin of His First Experiments on Combustion in 1772*, Cornell University Press, Ithaca 1961; Charles Coulston Gillispie, *The Montgolfier Brothers and the Invention of Aviation 1783-1784; With a Word on the Importance of Ballooning for the Science of Heat and the Art of Building Railroads*, Princeton Univ. Press, Ewing N.J. 1993; Georges Bataille, *The Accursed Share, vol.1*, Zone Books, New York 1989.

Kristin Feireiss talks to Wolf D. Prix
The Story of the Hurricane

The Tower of Babel, Pieter Bruegel the Elder, 1563

KRISTIN FEIREISS Parallel to the dynamic development of your career, you have given innumerable interviews in past years. Some of these were printed in the recent publication "Get Off of My Cloud," which features texts from your nearly forty years of work in architecture. To give a new interview now, there must be a good reason — and there is: the completion of BMW Welt in Munich. When we talk about this building today, the design process and its realization, we can't do so without touching on your previous oeuvre — your blueprints, buildings and extensive theoretical writings — all of which influenced BMW Welt in various ways. Let's start by talking about the year your office was founded, which makes you a genuine member of the 1968 generation. Your worldview ties you to this generation by virtue of the critical sociopolitical attitude you espouse and also apply to architecture. Borrowing a quote from Rudi Dutschke and replacing the word "society" with "architecture," you already wrote in 1970: "It's not up to us to change in order to live in architecture; architecture must respond to our movements, our feelings, our mood and our emotions so that we want to live in it." More than 30 years have gone by since then. Is this sentence still valid for you?

WOLF PRIX By all means! We've not only preserved the critical stance of the 1968 generation; what seems to me much more important is that we have also maintained the incredible optimism of those days. I think that unless you are an optimist you can never design and build architecture to fit the times. Back then, when we were young and just embarking on our careers, I had the notion that we had to change architecture immediately and radically, which is why I borrowed that line from Rudi Dutschke. We then realized, however, that circumstances in society and the social situation made rapid and radical transformation impossible. It has taken almost 40 years

for us to put into practice and build what we imagined back then. I think that if you start early enough and unfailingly follow your own path, it has to lead to success.

KRISTIN FEIREISS You and Coop Himmelb(l)au are an impressive illustration of this theory. This brings up the questions of how it all began: What role did the Tower of Babel play, an image you show in almost all of your lectures? Every architect surely dreams of completing this tower. What does it mean to you?

WOLF PRIX I'm not sure if every architect really would like to do that. I do think, though, that as an architect you should want to complete this tower. You could now justify this by citing the anti-authoritarian philosophy of the late 60s. But my personal story with regard to the Tower of Babel is a different one. My father was an architect. When I was a boy, he once took me to the Kunsthistorisches Museum in Vienna and showed me the painting by Pieter Bruegel. I was ten or eleven years old. I was thrilled by this picture, but it bothered me that the tower didn't have a spire, no roof. That's when I decided to become an architect. It's possible that this metaphor of completing a building appears again and again in my texts and drawings. But my decision to actually take up this career came later. My encounter with the work of Le Corbusier was the seminal moment. Visiting La Tourette was an overwhelming experience for me. I was so impressed and moved that I thought: "If that's architecture, then I want to make architecture." Naturally, I knew even then that it would take a long time to realize my dream. And because we knew that very well — and here is where the Tower of Babel comes in — we began with a detail out of the picture, namely the cloud. That was the occasion for founding Coop Himmelb(l)au. The text as well — that Himmelblau (sky blue) is not a color for us, but instead stands for architecture that changes like the clouds — comes from this idea. A great many of the projects we have executed were dictated by the cloud.

KRISTIN FEIREISS In 1968, the year you founded your architectural firm, you already translated this theoretical approach and the aspirations connected with it into reality in three projects: Villa Rosa I and Villa Rosa II, prototypes for a pneumatic residential unit and supply structure, and Wolke (cloud), a prototype for an organism for living.

WOLF PRIX We have always simply developed projects that interest us, something that is symptomatic for us and the way we work. We didn't need a contract in order to manifest our ideas. I think that is what sets us apart from young architects these days, who always wait for an assignment. Back then, we gave an answer before anyone asked a question — probably also an anti-authoritarian trait — and put our design ideas up for discussion. This was the case in the three projects just named, too. The question we asked ourselves was: What should architecture for our times look like?" What resulted was the development of pneumatic construction, which permits changes in volume using air as building material. This provides for modifiable forms, which have moveable platforms inside that allow room sequences and situations to be changed at will. The Wolke project was designed for the study "Residential Forms of the Future" and was worked out to the last detail in terms of structural engineering and construction.

KRISTIN FEIREISS A never-ending battle against gravity?

WOLF PRIX The suspension of gravity has always been a dream of architecture. Ever since the first totem pole was raised, demateri-

alization has been the goal. In architecture it begins with the Gothic cathedrals and can be traced through the Baroque period and on into our own era. Today, thanks to new construction methods that are easier to calculate using the computer, we are in a position to create buildings that come close to this dream of flying. The decisive factor here is that in suspending gravity, in weightless flight, which has become possible with the conquering of outer space, two things have been made manifest. First: with weightlessness there is no longer any central perspective, and second: the protective function as an architectural priority has been rendered obsolete by the spacesuit, which provides the human with the ideal form of protection. Even though some people are trying today to drive architecture into isolation with this insane philistine focus on catastrophes.

KRISTIN FEIREISS Isn't fear of terrorist attacks or natural disasters a basic existential anxiety?

WOLF PRIX Yes, but it's the wrong approach. It is absolutely no problem in the architecture of today to deal professionally with this challenge and to solve such matters by technical means. Responding to climate conditions and security aspects is simply a matter of course. Nevertheless, it is still strange how society is suddenly trying to reduce architecture to its original function as protective shell. The real catastrophe of the climate and the catastrophe of terror is for me as an architect what I call Taliban buildings: bunkers with slits. Insanely isolated.

KRISTIN FEIREISS It's not surprising that you take a position contrary to the commonly accepted one here as well. Let's talk about this for a moment. You once said, and this is also provocative, "Architecture

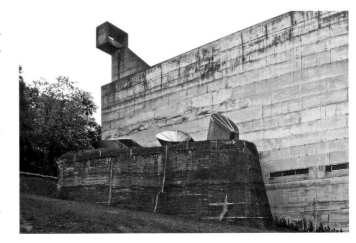

that is too accommodating is dangerous", and spoke in this context of the potential for indoctrination. What do you mean by an architecture that is accommodating? By what means does it indoctrinate?

WOLF PRIX "Accommodating" for me describes an architecture that prettifies, that does not put up any resistance and that therefore, once built, can immediately be forgotten again. This kind of architecture makes no contribution to the development of a society. It consists of buildings that cannot be read, that are simply boxes to fulfill a function, that hinder more than they liberate. Conformity and assimilation are always the expression of an opportunistic and entrenched attitude. Accommodating architecture indoctrinates because it freezes the status quo. Anything that generates changes is fought against. But life is all about change. If you don't change, you are dead.

KRISTIN FEIREISS The opposite of "accommodating architecture" is for you "non-conformist architecture" or a "non-conformist aesthetic."

WOLF PRIX A non-conformist aesthetic is also a political tool, because aesthetics that everyone expects, as I said, manifest the status quo. A non-conformist aesthetic is of course rejected at first, because it doesn't serve to camouflage problems but instead to generate a new consciousness. It's about architecture that is identifiable within this anonymous network of the city, and that puts new ideas up for discussion, ideas of about space, about function, about technology.

KRISTIN FEIREISS Where does your provocative potential come from? What is the source of your inexhaustible critical creativity?

WOLF PRIX I've always been able to think in terms of more than just architecture. Because if you only think about the architecture, then only architecture comes out. We were in a position to ponder the background behind social processes and how they come about and to incorporate architecture in these considerations, not the ideal world of architecture, because that no longer exists, but architecture as one of the most controversial themes of our age. This information is stored. I have it on my hard disk and that's why I keep looking behind the scenes and can see the big picture. That doesn't mean we are always against everything — on the contrary — but this overview enables us to bring our experience to bear on our urban planning and architectural concepts in order to develop new solutions.

KRISTIN FEIREISS In terms of the design process, you have never proceeded according to the usual European method — sketch, drawing, blueprint and finally presentation model. Sketch and working model have always been one in your design process. No presentation model, but conceptual models instead.

WOLF PRIX They are conceptual models. Two things are vital here: Architecture is a three-dimensional language that can only be spoken in three dimensions. I can't master it on paper. No matter how well you can imagine it, architecture on paper remains flat. To study it, I must transform it into the third dimension. That's one thing, the other is the design method, which has a philosophical background. At the moment of designing, we want to liberate space, which includes freeing it from material necessities, both economic and technical. This is why we have abbreviated the design process to include only the explosive moment. A sketch, a model: this is the point of departure for the development of a new building. I believe that this

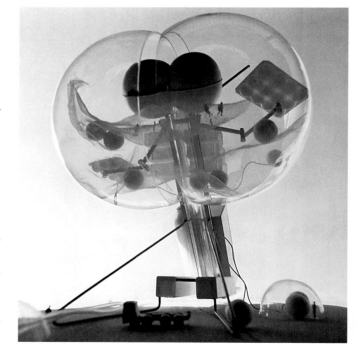

is the true deconstructivism that Derrida envisioned. He says that in every text *one* word, *one* sentence is written unconsciously to which the entire text then reacts. The blind white spot. It's the same way with architecture.

KRISTIN FEIREISS You once said: *Entwerfen kommt von Werfen.* (*Design comes from throwing:* The word for design in German, "entwerfen," contains the word "werfen" = to throw, *trans.*)

WOLF PRIX If you break down the word "Entwurf" (design), it is made up of the prefix "Ent" and the verb "werfen" (to throw). "Ent" conveys an unconscious process, such as in the words ent-flammen (catch fire), ent-äußern (divest oneself of), ent-tarnen (expose). "Werfen" clearly comes from the explosive moment of throwing. Both go together. Without knowing where it will take us, we begin to concentrate and shorten the time of the design (Entwurf) process. This moment, when you feel architecture, is the moment of design. This brought us to the realization that the freer the moment of design, the freer the architecture will be, even free from economic, technical and other material demands.

KRISTIN FEIREISS Your architecture, your formal vocabulary, has never been random. It has always been the transformation of your conceptual and philosophical approach into space. What is the form-giving means by which your architecture takes shape?

WOLF PRIX If I have an idea of a space, of a space that has not been built yet, then I know when I begin drawing this idea that there is always a technical construction that can translate this space into reality. It's always been that way, because we never said, "form follows function" or "function follows form." We have always assumed that

the two form a synergy. At the same time, construction as a supporting mainspring cannot be neglected. I can also put it this way: dynamic forces as form-giving means, as form-generating forces, have always been important to us. I'm thinking here for example of the rooftop remodeling on Falkestrasse in Vienna, where the metaphor of the thunderbolt opens up the rooftop and creates space, liberating the space so to speak. We showed that we could build that.

KRISTIN FEIREISS You've just spoken of dynamic forces. This book is also titled "Dynamic Forces." A coincidence?

WOLF PRIX No. This is just the next step in our architectural development, if I can put it that way. Dynamic forces have, as I said, always interested us, and me especially. The very early drawings show that the energy of the pencil stroke is an absolutely essential feature shaping our designs. Now we are in a position thanks to the computer and the new programs to realize this energy on a large scale as well. As we said back then: "The wind is a synonym for architecture," quoting Melville's "Would now the wind but had a body" — now we are one step further. Today, I can translate the metaphor of the dynamic power of a tornado into space; I can even let the forces of the wind itself shape the facade of a building.

KRISTIN FEIREISS Can you elaborate on that?

WOLF PRIX We always work, now more than ever, in a crossover system. So we build a model, digitize it, and then work on it on the computer. Wind and other forces can't be drawn; they must be simulated on the computer. Then another model is made and we rework the form using this model. So the building is not designed only on the computer. The computer can't simulate this process; it always takes

the third dimension of the model. Spatial, visual relationships, which always have an impact on form, also play a major role. This is a completely new development, in which I am personally very interested. We implemented this method in the roof of BMW Welt.

KRISTIN FEIREISS When you won the BMW competition, the project was still referred to as an entertainment and delivery center — now it has become a whole world: BMW Welt. What prompted you to take part in the competition? Did your enthusiasm for fast, high-tech cars have anything to do with it?

WOLF PRIX Yes, but I'm not an expert on cars — quite the opposite. I was fascinated by the Formula 1 racecars of the early years as marvels of technology and I've always said that architecture should be built like a Formula 1 racecar. But what really intrigued me about BMW Welt was to create an architectural language that adequately expresses this dynamism and elegance. A one-to-one transfer to architecture was not what I was interested in.

KRISTIN FEIREISS We've spoken about your sociopolitical attitude, which forms the basis for your oeuvre, as well as about the concept of non-conformist architecture, which can be applied to all Coop Himmelb(l)au buildings. With this fundamental attitude, how have you managed the balancing act of creating a building for BMW, one of the biggest automotive companies in the global market, a building that will shape this company's image worldwide? Can we still speak here of non-conformist architecture?

WOLF PRIX Naturally, BMW Welt serves to enhance the corporate image. But where is the difference between that and a Greek temple? It fulfilled the same function. It was a center of attraction and all

Genealogy of the roof

1973: The House with the Flying Roof, London, GB

1976: Super Sommer, Vienna, Austria

1998: JVC New Urban Entertainment Center, Guadalajara, Mexico

2001: BMW Welt, Munich, Germany

2002: Musée des Confluences, Lyon, France

around it a wide variety of activities crystallized, from schools to discussion forums and marketplaces. In a figurative sense, the same
goes for BMW Welt. The principle is an ancient one. What we do not
build, however, and we already made this clear in 1968, are nuclear
power plants, military facilities and prisons. Otherwise, I can imagine every kind of client. Incidentally, and this is something we also
formulated decades ago, we want our buildings to exert an influence
on what goes on there and even to stimulate processes of change.

KRISTIN FEIREISS A subversive strategy. Does the design for BMW
Welt also have subversive tendencies?
WOLF PRIX The aesthetic we have developed is directed against
authority and against hierarchy. When you convey dynamics and elegance by creating openness and BMW accepts that as a company
and doesn't immediately draw back in alarm, like for example clients
in the Arab countries might do because it doesn't match their own
principles of order, then this is a good basis for working together.

KRISTIN FEIREISS So a client has to accept your game rules, the
spatial rules ...
WOLF PRIX ... which make openness possible. By the way, that is
also what fascinated me about the competition. The not-very-con-
crete spatial program at the beginning gave us the opportunity to
create an open space. This was for me the first occasion to formulate a hybrid building in which several functions come together.

KRISTIN FEIREISS You like to speak in this connection of a functional
sculpture. A space that unites various functions, uses and activities
under one roof. This is definitely the case in BMW Welt. The building

is intended to form a setting for logistics and work processes, mar-
keting activities, the delivery of vehicles to the customers, galleries
and shops, a restaurant, an auditorium for large-scale events from
conferences to concerts. And all of this addresses different groups
of people: potential BMW customers and those who have already
purchased a car, BMW employees, and a public for which BMW Welt
represents an entertainment and leisure attraction. So it's a kind of
urban meeting place.
WOLF PRIX It is just like in a city. We deliberately did not separate
the various functions. We did not pack them away in their own buildings. Through the consolidation of these processes, room sequences emerged that are very exciting on the one hand and extremely
functional on the other. With us, the form and the program always
seesaw back and forth until they create a synergy resulting in a
readable, identifiable building.

KRISTIN FEIREISS Can BMW Welt be understood as a kind of stage
on which various actors perform?
WOLF PRIX We have created with BMW Welt a combination of theat-
er and marketplace, a building that through its spatial conception
also fulfills an urban purpose. The same goes incidentally for the
European Central Bank, which we are also in the process of building.
Various situations take place simultaneously on this stage. The im-
perative of interaction is in a certain sense a sociopolitical demand.
This is why we have a special penchant for multifunctional facilities.
We have always argued for the simultaneity of systems.

KRISTIN FEIREISS And all of this under one roof.
WOLF PRIX The realization of the roof, one that doesn't close off

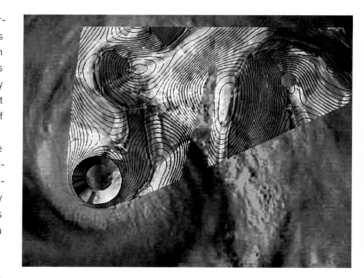

the space but instead opens it up, was fascinating for me, because it was the first time we were able to translate our ideas into space on this scale. We developed a sculptural roof as a space-differentiating element. The double cone out of which the roof emerges plays a central role here. Here I have to use free association. First image: I once watched my daughter twirling and observed how her bathrobe began to fly out to the sides. Through the dynamic of turning, part of the bathrobe begins to lift that otherwise clings to the body. At the same time, the enormous force exuded by a tornado came to mind. This is often seen only as destructive, but that isn't so. A tornado merely destroys artificially constructed obstacles.

KRISTIN FEIREISS   It is first and foremost a natural phenomenon.
WOLF PRIX   A natural phenomenon in which the dynamic forces lead to air turbulences of immense power and elegance. The double cone that comes about in this way has always thrilled me. This comes from an early model of the Firminy Church by Le Corbusier, where he constructs a cone over a rectangular floor plan in a fascinating way. The church was completed only recently according to his plans, near La Tourette. Our own exploration of this form began with an art project we did together with Kiki Smith. We used the double cone as stage setting for Peter Sellar's *Oedipus Rex*. The double cone is incidentally also present in the form of a cable construction in the UFA Cinema Center in Dresden. Here it is for the first time a true space. The construction underlines the dynamic and from this dynamic emerges the roof.

KRISTIN FEIREISS   Are there references to earlier projects in the development of the formal vocabulary for the roof of BMW Welt?

WOLF PRIX   In the roof conception, yes. In the form in which it has now been realized, no. One has to say, however, that since our Flying Roof of 1973, the roof has been a central theme for us. Lars Lerup makes a comparison in an essay between the different interests and working methods of individual architects when they build a house. Some, he writes, are interested only in the cellar vaults, some in the central block, and a very few design roofs. The latter, Lerup claims, can be considered part of the avant-garde. To me, Le Corbusier is one of them. His roofs are not roofs designed solely for protecting the building; they are, when I think of the example of La Tourette, landscapes — roof landscapes. The roof of BMW Welt is a reversed roof landscape by Le Corbusier. Do you understand?

KRISTIN FEIREISS   Can you explain that in more detail?
WOLF PRIX   In BMW Welt I didn't place the roof landscape atop the building, like Le Corbusier, but I flipped it, by 180 degrees. This yields a spatial differentiation that we used to place the required functions in certain places. We said: The roof determines the space, differentiates the space, and under this roof we will mentally install a stage that allows us to later place upon it the stage settings that are desired, the functions. That was, in short, the idea behind the design process for the BMW roof.

KRISTIN FEIREISS   Hearing you speak both analytically and emotionally about the design process involved in BMW Welt reminds me of how you once said: "The more intensely the design is experienced by the designer, the more intensely the built space will be experienced." It seems as though you experienced the design of BMW Welt extremely intensely.

WOLF PRIX The design process, particularly in the case of BMW Welt, is of course made up of many other complex influences besides those we have spoken of. The urban surroundings and the site of the building, for example, call for a response to the very strong spatial dominance of BMW headquarters: the Four Cylinders of the administration building and the shell of the BMW Museum. We had to come up with a very strong contemporary figure to respond to this extremely dominant architectural language. Our answer was the double cone, which, so to speak, stands at the intersection between the two existing buildings. This allowed us to take up the theme of dynamics in a logical fashion: the dynamics of traffic on one side of the building enters into a dialogue with the dynamics of the rotating double cone.

KRISTIN FEIREISS In terms of integrating BMW Welt into existing urban planning conditions, the spatial relationship to the Olympiapark and the television tower surely also play a pivotal role.

WOLF PRIX We carefully determined from where and how, for example, the Four Cylinders of the BMW tower are in view, from where the Olympiapark can be seen and from which points there is a glimpse of the roof of the Olympic stadium and the television tower. All of these sight lines were studied and analyzed and then summarized as a spatial continuum. The roof, for example, has a recess where the loggias are located in which BMW customers await delivery of their cars. From this gap, the Four Cylinders can be seen. Another very important aspect is that the building has two entrances: the main entrance on the side of company headquarters and an entrance from the subway station. This creates an attractive, generously proportioned passageway that immediately summons

the image of the Galleria in Milan: a divided arcade offering a variety of shops. Another urban planning element is the bridge that further underlines this connection. On the second level, visitors can use the bridge to access the double cone, or cross the street to reach the museum. The building is networked in several directions. It has many views and perspectives.

KRISTIN FEIREISS The principle of openness is carried forward into the outside space. A city landscape?

WOLF PRIX In the figurative sense, a landscape is describable and a city, in order to be experienced, must likewise be describable, which it becomes when it features identifiable buildings. BMW Welt fulfills both. Inside and outside. What I understand under the term cityscape is of course more mixed. The grid-patterned mental space. This is also shown by the image we use of the chessboard. When we are asked how architecture should look today, I like to invoke the example of the chessboard where the playing pieces are caught in checkmate. That is the architecture, but the checkerboard pattern, the black-and-white squares, will later be dissolved. What remains is the architecture, and it has to be as strong as the pieces on the chessboard, in which you can still read and sense their moves — architecture must have the same power, the same radiance.

KRISTIN FEIREISS After everything we've already talked about, I still have one question: What do you regard as the most essential element of your architecture? Is there one?

WOLF PRIX I think it is the fourth dimension of architecture: time. The time we need to walk through a building plays an important role in how we perceive the space.

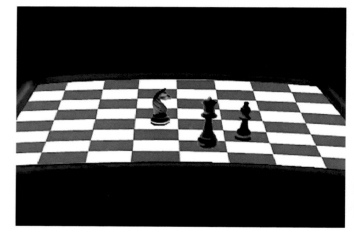

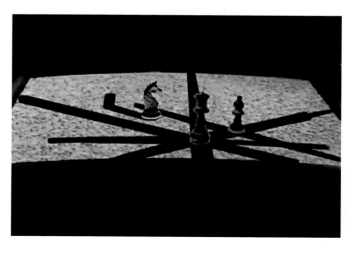

KRISTIN FEIREISS   The penetration of the body into space. To come back to the space in BMW Welt, it is clear that this space cannot be taken in at one glance — is that due to the dimensions?

WOLF PRIX   No, it's because of the various perceptual levels and different spatial sequences. You must wander through the building in order to comprehend all of the different sight lines and space sequences. BMW Welt is certainly not what you might call a one-liner, a building that can be taken in all at once, that can be immediately comprehended. That would be like me describing Shakespeare's *Hamlet* as follows: Hamlet learns of the murder of his father, stabs his uncle to death and dies. The fact is that, in Shakespeare, whom I greatly admire, several different stories are always interwoven. In Shakespeare they are hybrid stories, in our case they are hybrid spaces; neither can be decoded at a glance: you must penetrate them. Architecture demands an open awareness.

KRISTIN FEIREISS   You once said, "Architecture can stage a better future," and you wrote, "With our architecture we want to give people the feeling that they are free and unfettered, free to act." That could have come straight out of a manifesto written by the "Gläserne Kette" group, who were convinced as early as the start of the last century that architecture could make an essential contribution to changing society and improving each individual's living conditions. Do you feel misunderstood when people call you a visionary or, as Heinrich Klotz put it, a "realistic utopian"?

WOLF PRIX   Let's put it this way, in the words of Che Guevara: "Let's be realists — and do the impossible." That's great, isn't it?

Competition

After reviewing initial concepts back in 1997, the BMW Group decided in 2000 to build a center for brand experience and automobile delivery (working title at the time: BMW Experience and Delivery Center) where customers from all over the world could come to pick up their new BMW car in person and in the process be treated to an unforgettable live experience of the BMW brand. After various location alternatives had been considered, it was soon clear that the ideal site for the project could only be in physical and psychological proximity to the world-renowned high-rise — company headquarters — and the BMW Museum.

A parking garage from the 1970s would have to be demolished to make room for BMW Welt at the birthplace of the BMW brand, the former "Oberwiesenfeld". The location could not have been better. This is historic ground for BMW. The northern edge of the Oberwiesenfeld airfield is where Gustav Otto began in 1911 to produce airplanes in his "flying-machine factory", while Karl Rapp was building aircraft engines here in his "motor works" from 1913. In several stages, these two companies would ultimately become the Bavarian Motor Works.

BMW Welt was intended as an architectural landmark representing the heart of the BMW brand, a structure that would lastingly shape the client's corporate identity. The mission was both a complex and exceptional one. This is why the competition was preceded by an application procedure open to international contenders. From the 275 submissions received, 28 candidates were shortlisted for the second phase. From this moment on, the competition became a cooperative process in which at an unusually early stage an intensive dialogue was conducted between the architects and the client.

Following this second competition phase, a jury of professionals and BMW board members awarded the third prize to Morphosis Architects of Los Angeles and second prize to Zaha Hadid Architects of London.

The two first-prize winners, Coop Himmelb(l)au and the architect team of Sauerbruch/Hutton from Berlin, were invited to revise their plans with respect to technical, economic and functional aspects. Coop Himmelb(l)au came out the winner.

The competition plot is situated to the east of the BMW high-rise, in an industrial area marked primarily by the BMW Munich factory. Further to the east and south, a mixed residential area borders the site. To the west are the outdoor facilities of the Olympiapark with the Olympic Stadium. The competition specifications offered the possibility of conceptually interconnecting what had until then usually been strictly separate usage areas at the border between different urban structures.

Adding a new chapter to the industrially shaped history of the location, which was to maintain this character in the future, an individual building would now join the predominately mixed-use areas to the north and east, and the recreational facilities at Olympiapark — a building that would bring together many different functions and thus act as a catalyst for future developments at this site. Apart from the necessity of tying the new building into the urban planning context and the Olympiapark ensemble, another significant part of the assignment was to connect the various building functions in such a way that could all be reached on foot, assuming a usage volume of up to 900,000 visitors per year.

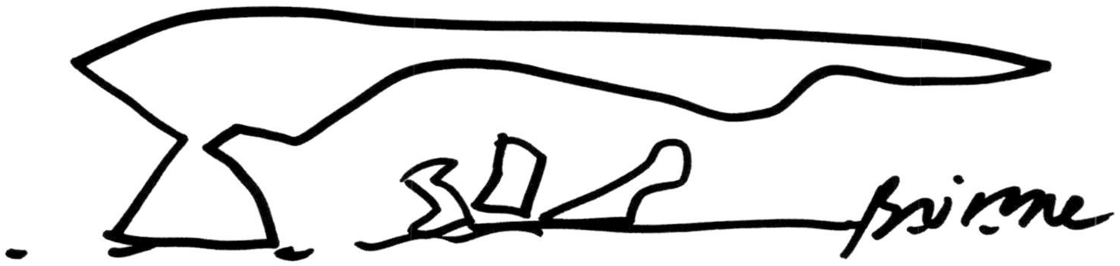

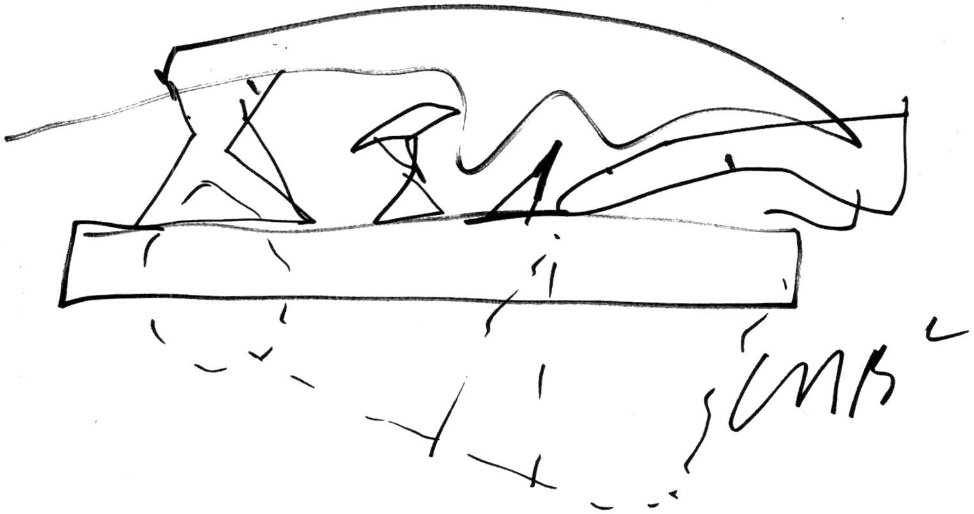

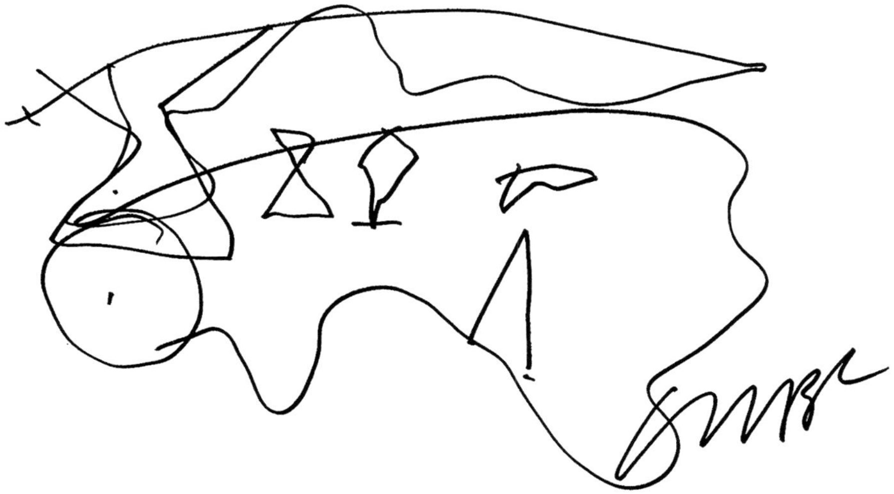

Phase 1

One of the central ideas in the plan was to merge the pre-existing buildings, the BMW high-rise and museum, with a further element in order to create a spatial and conceptual unity that would provide an identity. The theme of the flowing landscape, as well as those of cloud, double cone, ramps and bridges, became constitutive elements of the design even during the first planning phase. Vehicle delivery, the auditorium and other self-contained functional units were consistently provided for within the roof structure. The landscape that would emerge beneath the cloud roof would be allocated flexibly based on a checkerboard grid. The imposing vertical development of the building, including the exit ramps for the new vehicles, was to be realized by way of the Double Cone.

Phase 2

In this phase, the basic urban planning concept was maintained while the large, multifunctional Hall was modified in terms of both function and structure, with its various space-defining elements fused into a continuous series of rooms. The roof, or cloud, was to a great extent relieved of functional areas in favor of a more economical construction method and a building skin optimized according to aspects of ecology and the layout of technical facilities. The roof took on the functions of air supply and ventilation, of cooling, energy production and lighting that could be regulated and modified to create variable moods. Only the Lounge area is now encapsulated within the roof structure. The Premiere, or vehicle delivery area, was relocated to ground-floor level. The dimensions of the Hall were enlarged. Due to the sculptural roof, room heights ranged from 8 to 20 meters. The wedge-shaped indentations in the roof volume afforded sight lines within the building and toward the outdoors that were important for communication.

Phase 3

The third phase was marked above all by the structural and functional elaboration of the second-phase concept in order to ensure technical and economic feasibility. The event area in the Forum became a building-within-the-building. In order to optimize the organization of vehicle delivery, the traffic areas were reduced.

Phase 1: March — May 2001

Phase 2: June — July 2001

Phase 3: August — September 2001

  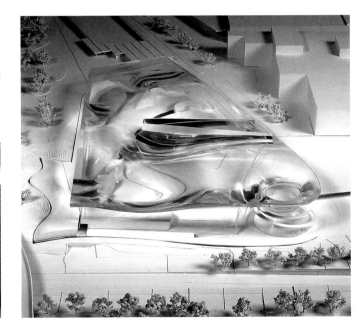

Phase 1

Concept model, competition, phase 1, scale 1:1000, April 2001

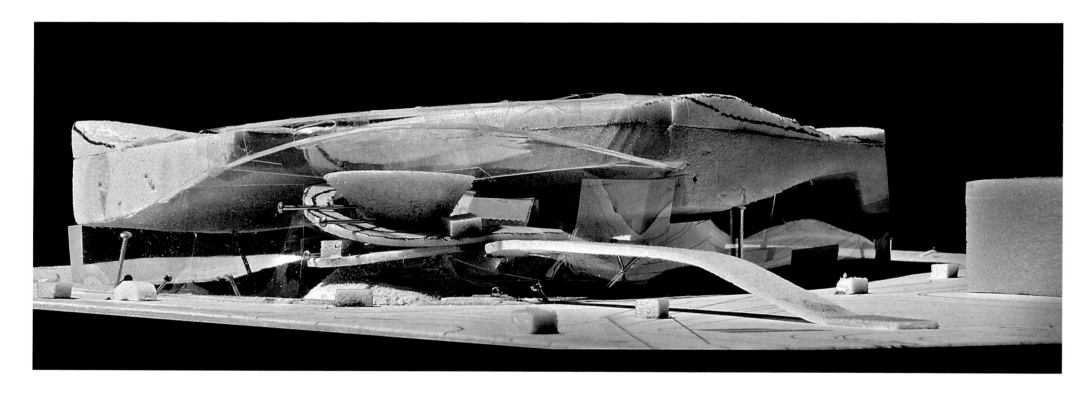

Concept model, "inverse landscape", scale 1:500, April 2001
Below: longitudinal section, draught, phase 1, "vehicle transfer in roof", May 2001

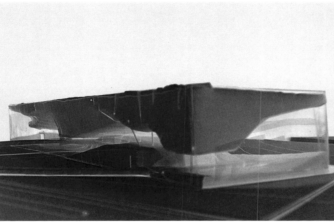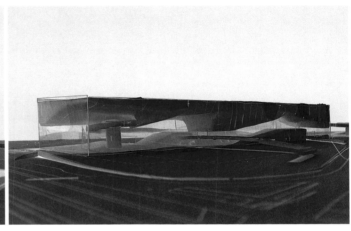

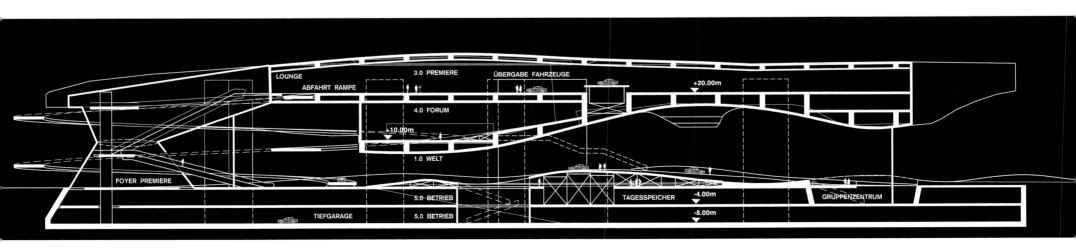

Phase 2

Concept model, competition, phase 2, June 2001
Below: South aspect, competition, phase 2, July 2001

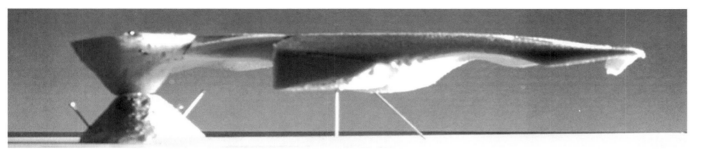

South aspect, competition, phase 2, July 2001

Phase 3

Ground plan, level E0, competition, phase 3, September 2001

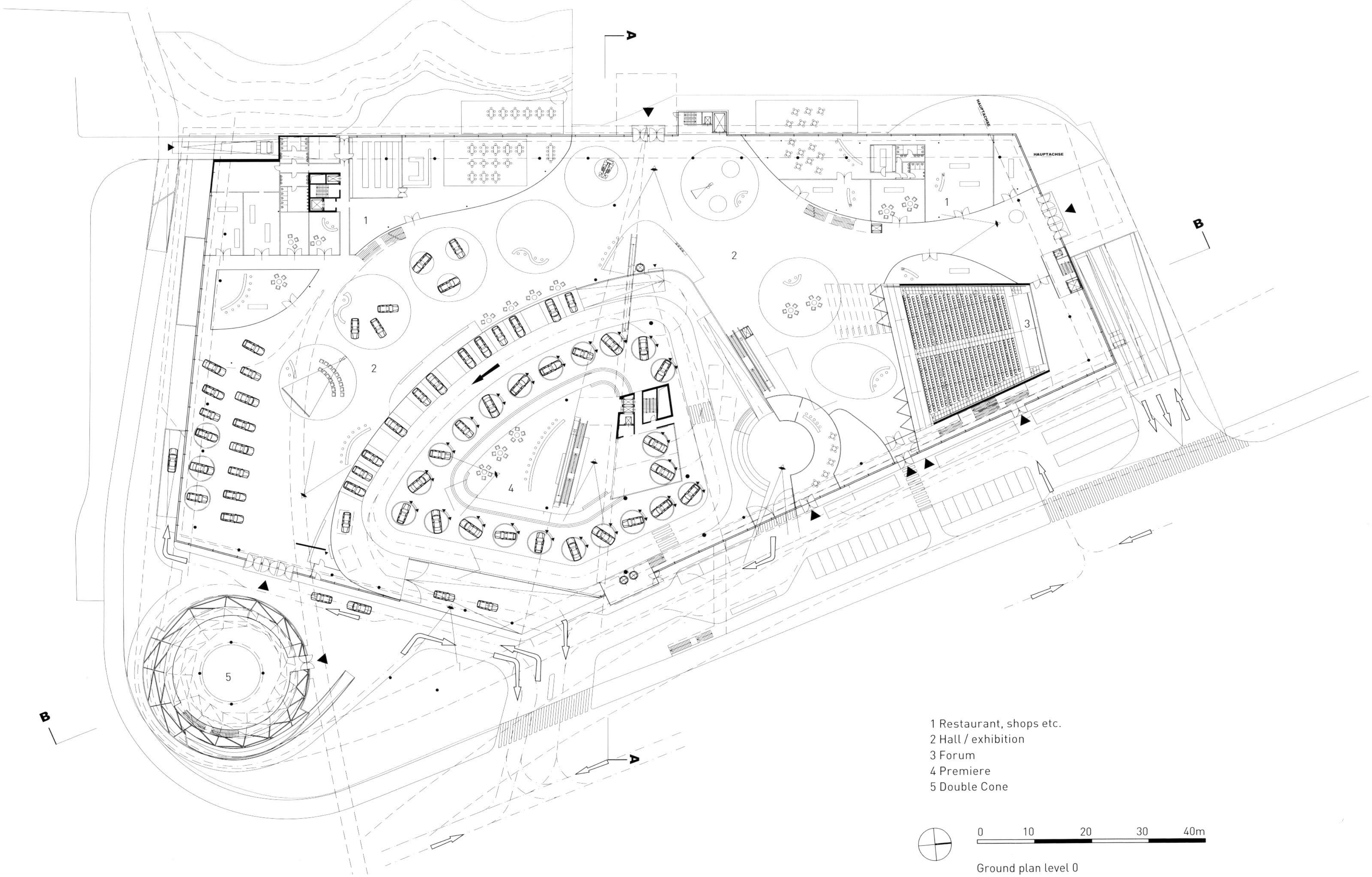

1 Restaurant, shops etc.
2 Hall / exhibition
3 Forum
4 Premiere
5 Double Cone

Ground plan level 0

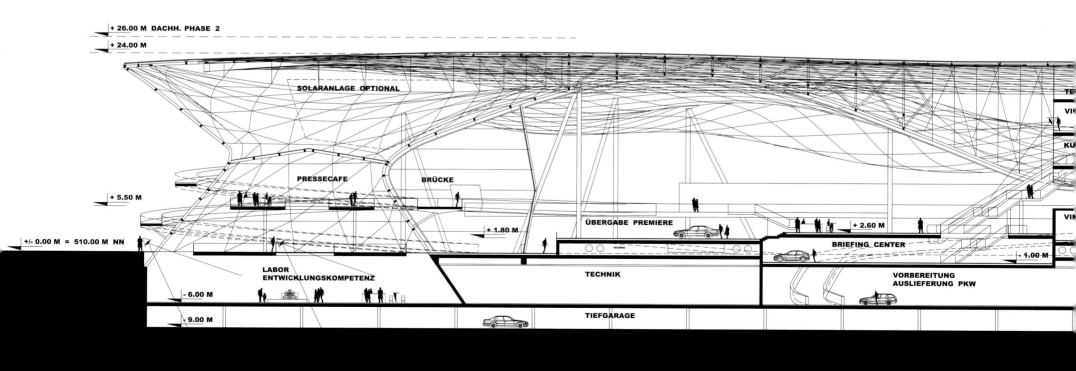

+ 26.00 M DACHH. PHASE 2

+ 24.00 M

SOLARANLAGE OPTIONAL

PRESSECAFE   BRÜCKE

+ 5.50 M

ÜBERGABE PREMIERE

+ 1.80 M

+ 2.60 M

+/- 0.00 M = 510.00 M NN

BRIEFING CENTER

- 1.00 M

LABOR
ENTWICKLUNGSKOMPETENZ

TECHNIK

TECHNIK

VORBEREITUNG
AUSLIEFERUNG PKW

- 6.00 M

- 9.00 M

TIEFGARAGE

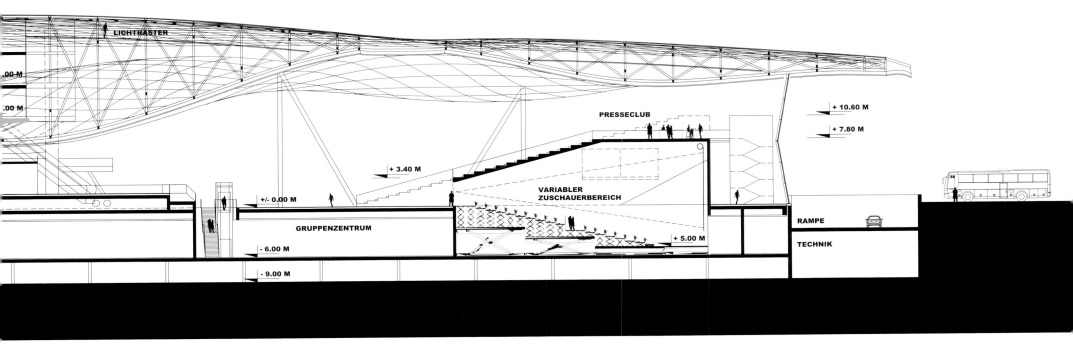

Longitudinal section, competition, phase 3, September 2001

LICHTRASTER

PRESSECLUB

+ 10.60 M

+ 7.80 M

+ 3.40 M

VARIABLER
ZUSCHAUERBEREICH

+/- 0.00 M

GRUPPENZENTRUM

RAMPE

- 6.00 M

+ 5.00 M

TECHNIK

- 9.00 M

In fact. From the very start …

Would now the wind but had a body, but all the things that most exasperate and outrage mortal man, all these things are bodiless, but only bodiless as objects, not as agents. There's a most special, a most cunning, oh, a most malicious difference!
(from: *Moby Dick* by Herman Melville)

HAMLET: *Do you see yonder cloud that's almost in shape of a camel?*
POLONIUS: *By th' mass, and 'tis like a camel indeed.*
HAMLET: *Methinks it is like a weasel.*
POLONIUS: *It is backed like a weasel.*
HAMLET: *Or like a whale.*
POLONIUS: *Very like a whale.*
(from: *Hamlet* by William Shakespeare,
Scene 2, A hall in the castle)

In fact. From the very start we've wanted to build cloud architectures and cities that change like banks of clouds. Because I feel that the sentence from Herman Melville's *Moby Dick*: "Would now the wind but had a body," is the best description of architecture. It was back in 1968, when we wanted to change architecture right away, and radically. Grown more patient through experience, we realized that back then with our "right away" we had over- or underestimated the effects of politics, clients and the prevailing concept of the aesthetic of form. Back then.

The strategy of taking small steps has always been alien to me. I think more in terms of the "step by step" you might take wearing seven-league boots.

"Would now the wind but had a body": Dynamic forces as space, drafting paradigms and transforming the structure from a static into a dynamic one …

Today, everything is conceivable, and depicting daring architecture in colorful announcements is easy. But what is still radical is wresting these images from a one-dimensional illustration and pushing them through — and realizing them — in three dimensions. Radical architecture is only radical today when it is also built … that is the difference between now and then.

The play of dynamic forces in nature has always inspired us and sometimes even provided a model for liberating the space (the architecture) from gravity, because architecture is also, as could already be read in the Gothic cathedrals, the dream of flying weightlessly through space. Bigger than life.

Building with air in the 1960s allowed us to conceive huge unsupported spaces for architecture, spaces that change like the clouds.

But it was not until we developed a design method that enabled us to investigate a new space by means of drawings and models, and then to convert it into three-dimensional language using the new tool of the computer, that it was possible for us to develop new forms and new structures for hybrid spaces. The competition for BMW Welt gave us the opportunity to examine these ideas in the wind channel of reality and to put them into practice.

One might compare the evolution of the BMW Welt project from concept to execution with a spatially complex puzzle. With ongoing feedback from our client, BMW AG, we designed a building that people can experience as a condensed city center.

The concept behind the design envisions a hybrid building representing a mixture of urban elements. Not an exhibition hall, not an information and communication center, not a museum, but instead all of these things, along a passage organized under one roof and horizontally and vertically layered. A conjoining of urban marketplace and stage for presentations.

One could perhaps compare it to the Acropolis in Athens, which as a city landmark was not only a temple but also marketplace, meeting place and information center. The urban planning idea was to place next to BMW headquarters, whose emblem is the four-cylinder tower and the museum shell, a third icon in step with the times, which would form an ensemble with the existing buildings despite the road separating them. The Double Cone, which in the design became a dynamic element, is the point of origin for a roof that, resting on only eleven columns, sculpturally configures the gigantic space and, by means of vertical differentiation, creates zones in the interior that can be experienced as spatial sequences. Views open up the building from the inside to the outside world and

from the outside inward — a cut-out in the roof connects BMW Welt visually with the four-cylinder tower, and the bridge literally connects and extends the interior formal vocabulary to the outside.

Ever since Le Corbusier liberated the roof of the Unité from its narrow definition as protective lid and turned it into a landscape, and since Oscar Niemeyer's design for the single-family home "Casa das Canoas" near Rio de Janeiro, we have realized that the roof does not have to follow the floor plan. The ROOF has taken on a new meaning in modern architecture.

Hybrid buildings that are more than mere functional shells are the building blocks of the city, a city of the future. Because when they are publicly accessible they are more than just a trademark of the company that built them. They represent added value for the city, re-interpreting the concept of public space. In the anonymous fabric of the city they are identification points, like figures on a chessboard that have traded the black-and-white grid for the white noise of the information society. Even though the urban planning grid has been dissolved, the figures and the force or energy of their moves can still be read.

Check!

Wolf D. Prix, 2007

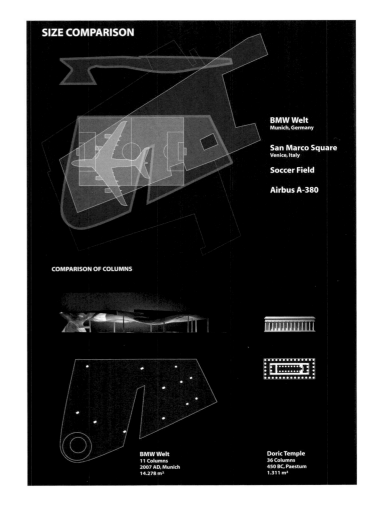

SIZE COMPARISON

BMW Welt
Munich, Germany

San Marco Square
Venice, Italy

Soccer Field

Airbus A-380

COMPARISON OF COLUMNS

BMW Welt
11 Columns
2007 AD, Munich
14.278 m²

Doric Temple
36 Columns
450 BC, Paestum
1.311 m²

Plinth model, scale 1:43, with back-lighting
Premiere
Forum

Bridge
Roof seen from below showing course of joins in panelling
Tower

Double Cone, shell from 3D moulding cutter, direct from 3D CAD model
Facades
Lounge

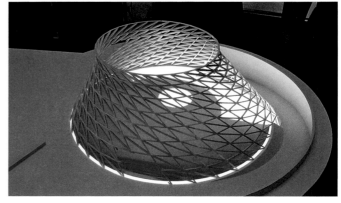

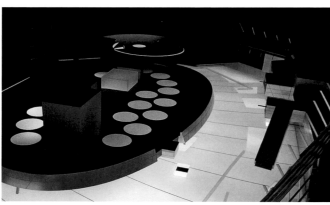

It is only the development of the design method, which allows us to explore a new space by means of a drawing and model, and to combine it with the new tool of the computer as a three-dimensional language, that enables us to develop new forms and new structures for hybrid spaces.

Model: view of roof from below and gravity wave in the Double Cone, scale 1:43

Elevator core with supports for Lounge, scale 1:43
Staircase
Helical staircase, Double Cone

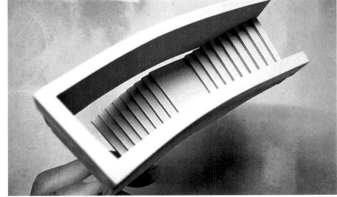

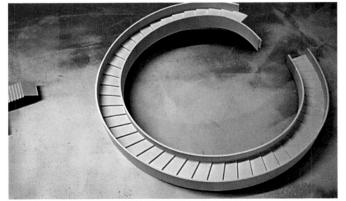

Spatial and Functional Concept

While analyzing the spatial and functional concept, it rapidly became apparent that BMW Welt could not be based on a classic monofunctional building typology. Not only were diverse, heterogeneous functions to be housed in a single building; these functions were also meant to complement and interact with one another, while also functioning as a building within a building if necessary. Which typology came closest to meeting these requirements?

As in a museum, special routing was needed to create a dramaturgical unfolding, but at the same time a stage-like space that offered maximum flexibility for constantly changing productions and events. In parallel, the building was also to function as a public communication platform — a marketplace — and with an almost church-like succession of spaces showcase the products and identity of the client. The sum of the individual typologies makes BMW Welt special.

The interplay of the various functional areas and the fact that BMW Welt, as a freestanding building, could have no hidden rear section posed unforeseen challenges to the planning team. The spatial and functional program, which took up around 45,000 square meters in the competition, grew in the ensuing planning phases to cover a total of more than 75,000 square meters. The reasons for this lay only in part in an expansion of the range of uses. The complexity of the various processes taking place simultaneously in the building can best be compared to several plays running parallel. Each of these events needs its own stage, but also its own backstage and auxiliary rooms.

At a very early phase, the processes in BMW Welt had to be coordinated with the widely networked logistics processes of BMW AG in order to define quantity and quality of use. For example, in order to guarantee punctual vehicle delivery, the entire production process

at the BMW plants had to be switched over from scheduling deliveries for a certain week to pinpointing an exact day. A growth in floor space of over 50 percent with a non-modifiable plot size and a maximum building height in accordance with urban planning regulations led to a tremendous consolidation and overlapping of the various functional areas. What was conceived in the competition as a vast covered hall with structurally freestanding pavilions inserted onto a checkerboard grid, became in the course of planning a diversely networked spatial city.

Special priority was placed on free sight lines and visual interaction between the various areas within BMW Welt as well as with the building's immediate surroundings. The transparent glass facades permit views of the landscape of the Olympiapark from inside the building. The Four Cylinders building designed by Karl Schwanzer, headquarters of the BMW Group, is honored with a special gesture: a wedge cut out of the roof shape. Through this gap the entire high-rise can be experienced from within BMW Welt at certain points in the process of vehicle delivery.

At the heart of BMW Welt is vehicle delivery, which forms both the spatial hub and the functional backbone of the building, and the processes connected with this function extend over almost all levels. The new vehicles are delivered to the lower floors via their own loading yard. Here there are carwashes, mechanics' workshops, final paint inspection sites and final cleaning sites as well as a one-day storage facility, an automatic high-rise storage unit with a capacity for 250 cars. This corresponds to the maximum daily capacity of the vehicle delivery process.

The delivery and end-finish process takes place hidden from customers and visitors on an underground stage. The vehicles are then transported in transparent glass elevators to the actual delivery stage, dubbed "Premiere," which is at the center of BMW Welt, visible from all other areas. This area is also known as the "Marina" since the vehicles are handed over to customers on rotating platforms, from where they can drive out of the building via a generously sized ramp.

Although BMW Welt is basically a public building, certain areas are open exclusively to those picking up new vehicles. For example, at the main entrances to BMW Welt customers can check into a hotel and enjoy exclusive use of two Lounge levels. The Lounge is integrated into the roof and thus virtually suspended over the delivery area, supported only by the utility service shafts and a column.

The necessary formalities for vehicle hand-over are taken care of in the Lounge, which also contains common areas where guests who have arrived from far away can withdraw and rest. Via a gradually descending stairway connecting the Lounge to the Marina, the customer is guided by a customer service representative to the actual hand-over point. In this process the melding of interior and exterior space or suspension of the usual separation between them also becomes tangible on the functional level.

Another key function of BMW Welt is represented by the Forum. Located in the north wing of the building, this section embodies in a particularly striking way the concept of spatial and visual integration coupled with the highest degree of functional independence. The heart of the Forum is an Auditorium for up to 800 persons. Equipped with a variable topography of hydraulic platforms, it can be used for a variety of events, from the annual BMW AG financial press conference to classic theater pieces. Via a liftable gate that can be sunk

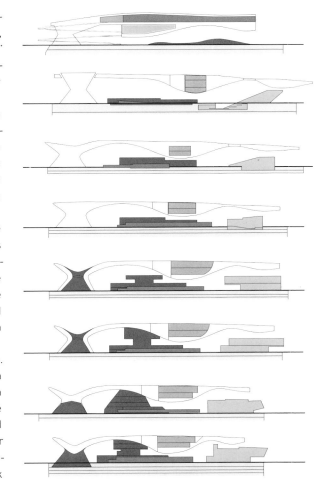

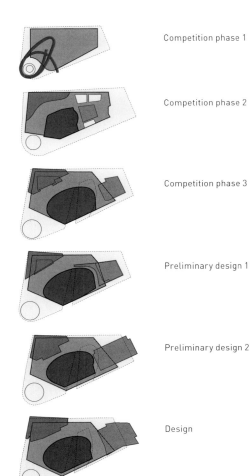

Competition phase 1

Competition phase 2

Competition phase 3

Preliminary design 1

Preliminary design 2

Design

into the floor across the entire width of the stage space, the Forum can be connected with the Hall to create a new kind of grand-scale event space.

The Auditorium was realized as a "space within a space" in acoustic terms, meaning that when the liftable gate is closed, no sound permeates from the Auditorium to the Hall or vice-versa. This makes it possible to hold functionally autonomous events simultaneously in the Hall and in the directly adjacent conference area. The Forum is supplemented by a full-service conference area, which is cantilevered out over 20 meters from the building block of the Forum, dominating the vista toward the north. The conference rooms can be adapted for various situations using mobile dividing walls. The section of the Forum structure visible "above ground" is only the tip of the iceberg. On the lower floors, the Forum includes a truck loading dock, catering kitchens, artists' dressing rooms and interpreter booths as well as storage spaces and service rooms, which together account for twice the space of the actual core areas.

The Tower in the southwest, looking toward the Olympiapark, represents a multifunctional area in the fullest sense of the term. Just like the Forum, it offers both encapsulated interior rooms with sight lines out into the Hall and toward the Olympiapark as well as walk-through surfaces and terraces both indoors and outdoors. In addition to the two main restaurant units, it also includes exhibition and sales floors as well as the administrative offices with workplaces for up to 200 persons and the Junior Campus for children and young people. Like the Forum, this structure requires widely branching roots in the lower stories. All the supply and disposal systems run through a loading yard assigned to this area, supplemented by storage areas, coat checks and staff rooms.

Special attention was paid to the underground networking of the various structures, so that it is possible to provide catering and supplies to the entire building from all restaurant units. The four-story underground base of BMW Welt also contains two public parking levels with up to 600 parking spaces. Access to the Hall is gained decentrally via 16 elevator groups. These underground service areas at BMW Welt cover 48,000 square meters, double the floor area of the aboveground levels, which comes to about 28,000 square meters including the auxiliary rooms.

In its functional multiplicity the Double Cone is no less impressive than the structures described above. It, too, is a full-service event realm extending over several levels, including a stage with its own catering infrastructure, rotating platforms and infrastructure connections for events such as concerts, exhibitions and talk shows. The Double Cone also makes it possible to exhibit vehicles from the workshop area. All of these structures take the form of walk-through sculptures in an urban landscape that is overarched by the virtually free-floating roof that originates out of the Double Cone and further differentiates the space into various sub-areas.

Inside BMW Welt, all publicly accessible areas, such as the Forum, Tower and Double Cone, are connected by a lightweight, sweeping bridge structure. In order to eliminate columns in the interior, the bridge was hung from the ceiling instead. At defined panorama points, curving bulges in the bridge invite guests to pause and take in the scene.

The functional and formal concept of the bridge is extended out over Lerchenauerstrasse and thus to BMW areas situated on the opposite side of the street (administration headquarters and museum), so there is no intersection with the vehicle traffic down below.

Axonometric depiction of the
functional processes

0 — 0   Sequence of functions

Visitor routes

VIP routes

Customer routes

Deliveries

Links with works

Premiere

VIP Premiere

Forum

Catering area

Car-park

Works

Double Cone

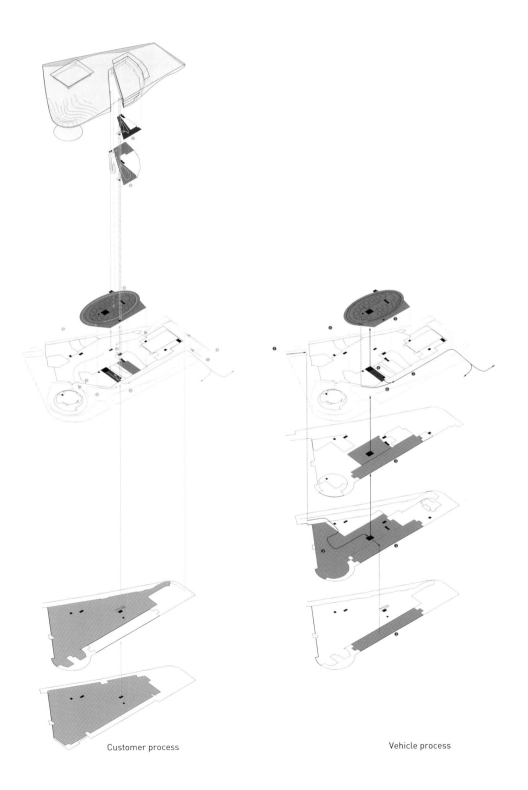

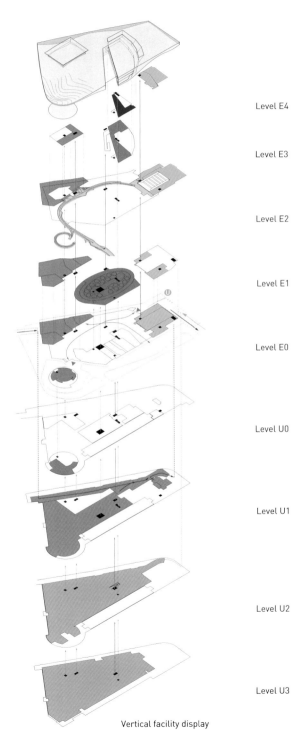

Level E4

Level E3

Level E2

Level E1

Level E0

Level U0

Level U1

Level U2

Level U3

Customer process   Vehicle process   Vertical facility display

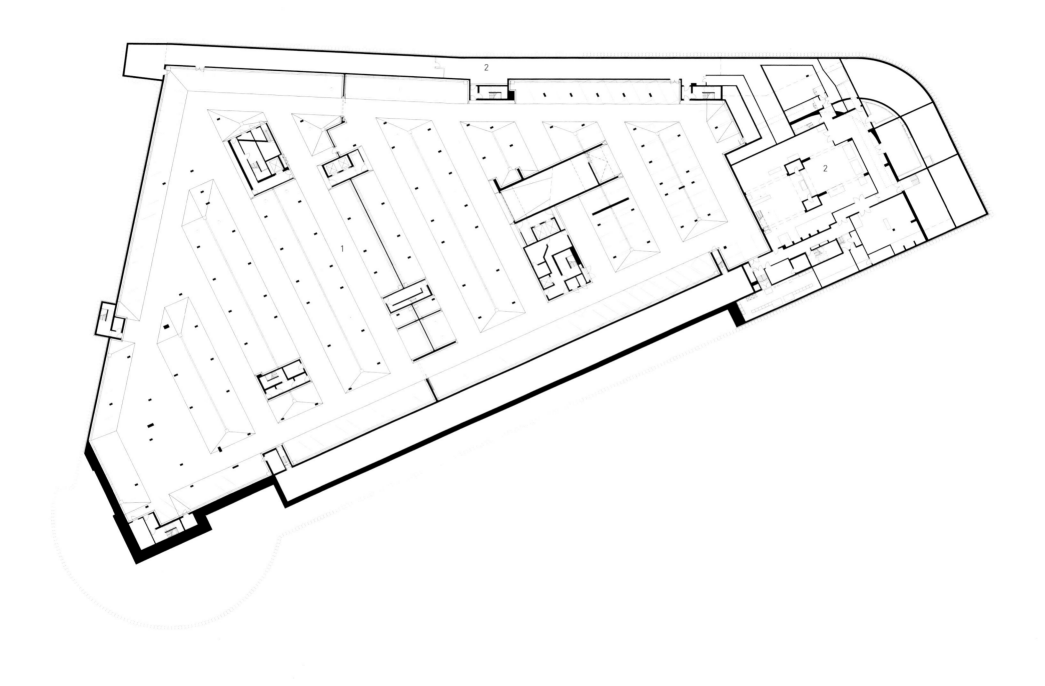

Ground plan level U3

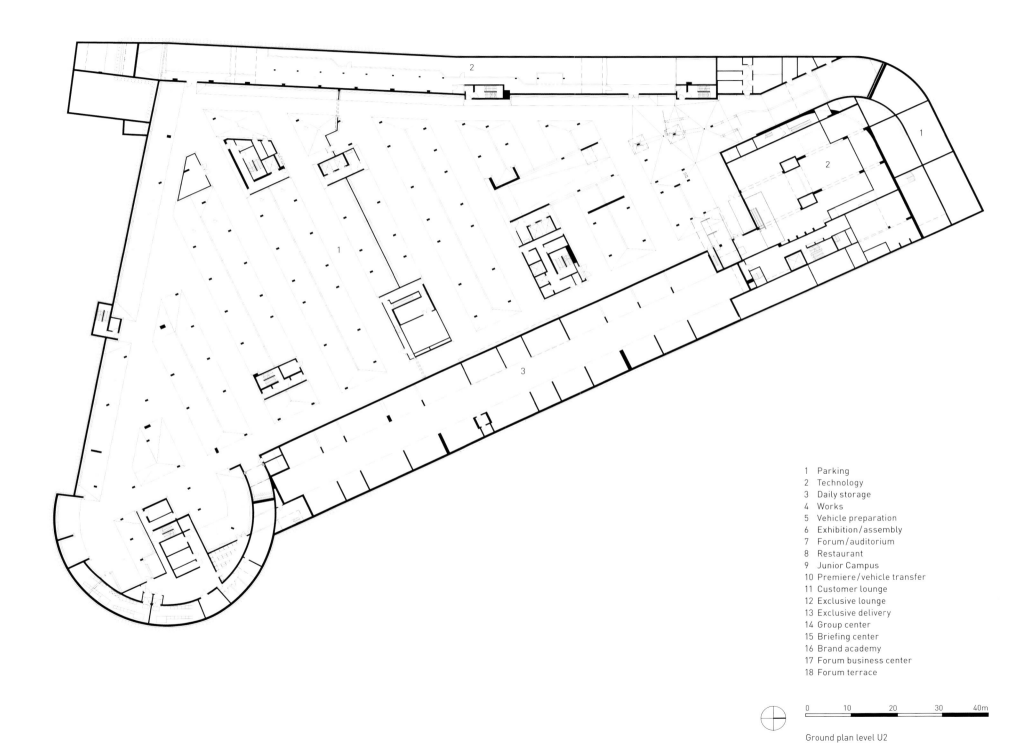

1 Parking
2 Technology
3 Daily storage
4 Works
5 Vehicle preparation
6 Exhibition/assembly
7 Forum/auditorium
8 Restaurant
9 Junior Campus
10 Premiere/vehicle transfer
11 Customer lounge
12 Exclusive lounge
13 Exclusive delivery
14 Group center
15 Briefing center
16 Brand academy
17 Forum business center
18 Forum terrace

0   10   20   30   40m

Ground plan level U2

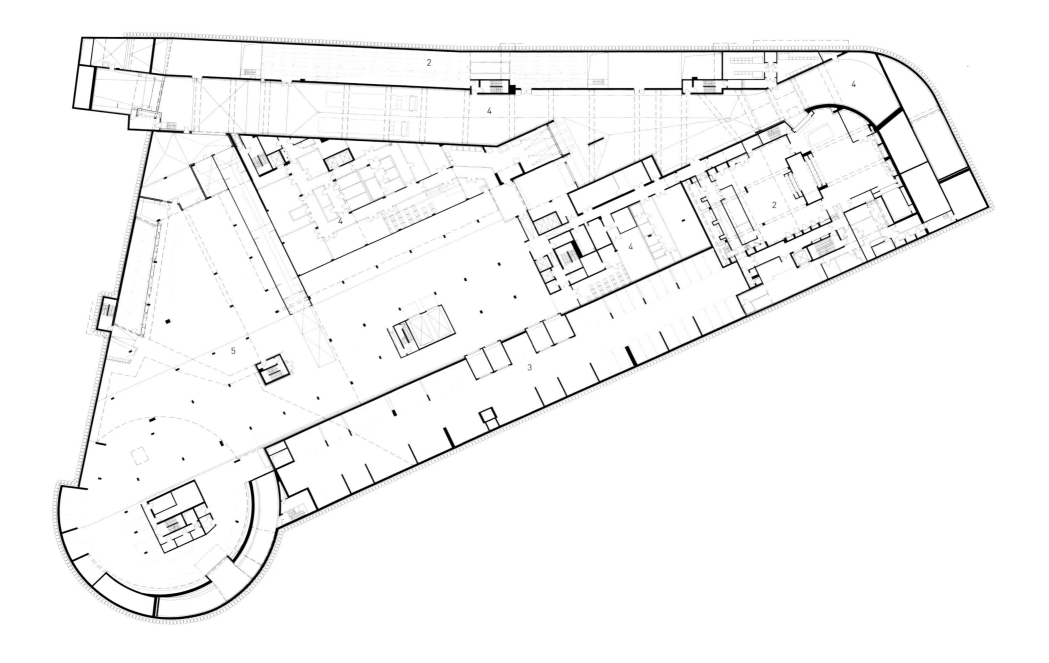

2

4

4

4

4

2

4

5

3

| 0 | 10 | 20 | 30 | 40m |

Ground plan level U1

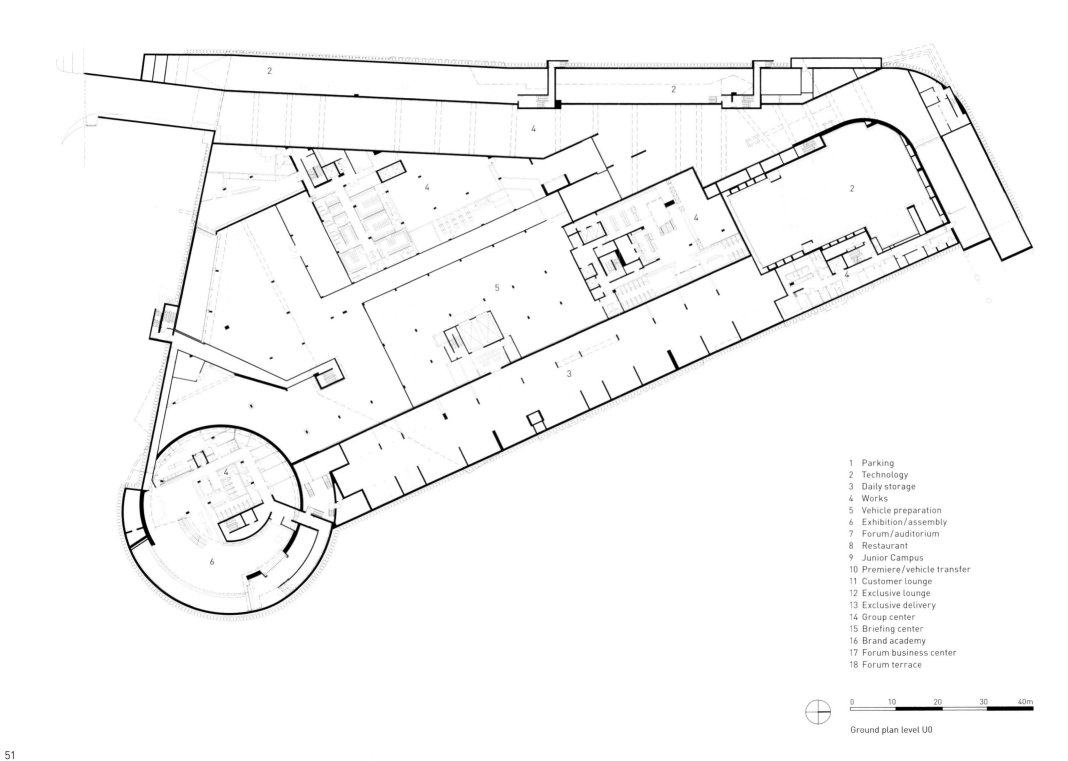

1 Parking
2 Technology
3 Daily storage
4 Works
5 Vehicle preparation
6 Exhibition/assembly
7 Forum/auditorium
8 Restaurant
9 Junior Campus
10 Premiere/vehicle transfer
11 Customer lounge
12 Exclusive lounge
13 Exclusive delivery
14 Group center
15 Briefing center
16 Brand academy
17 Forum business center
18 Forum terrace

0   10   20   30   40m

Ground plan level U0

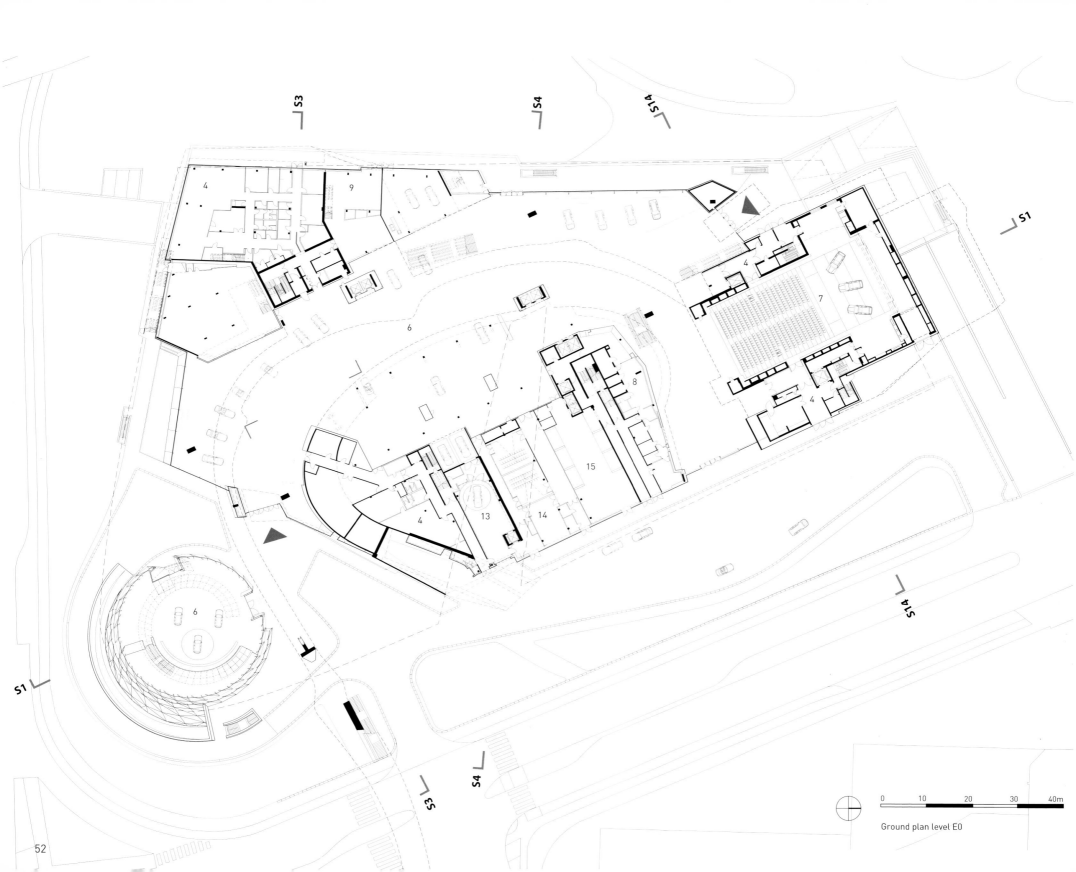

S3   S4   S14

S1

4   9

4

7

6

8

15

4   13   14

S14

6

S1

S3   S4

0   10   20   30   40m

Ground plan level E0

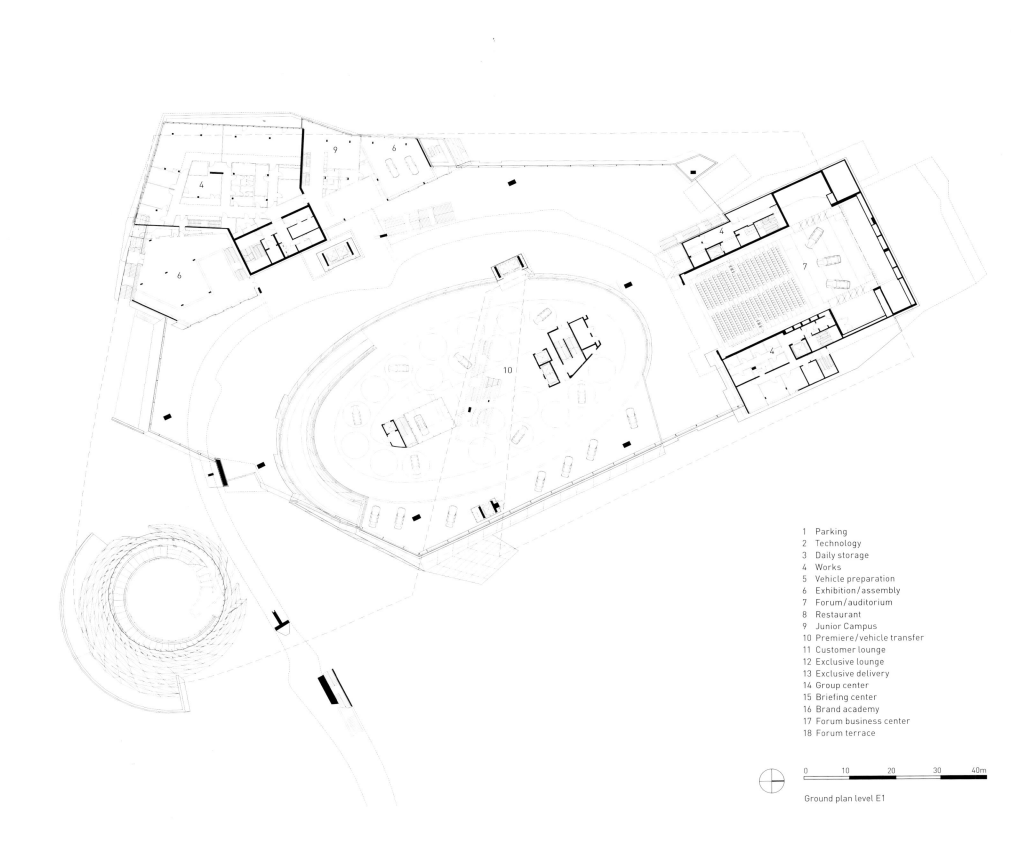

1   Parking
2   Technology
3   Daily storage
4   Works
5   Vehicle preparation
6   Exhibition/assembly
7   Forum/auditorium
8   Restaurant
9   Junior Campus
10   Premiere/vehicle transfer
11   Customer lounge
12   Exclusive lounge
13   Exclusive delivery
14   Group center
15   Briefing center
16   Brand academy
17   Forum business center
18   Forum terrace

0   10   20   30   40m

Ground plan level E1

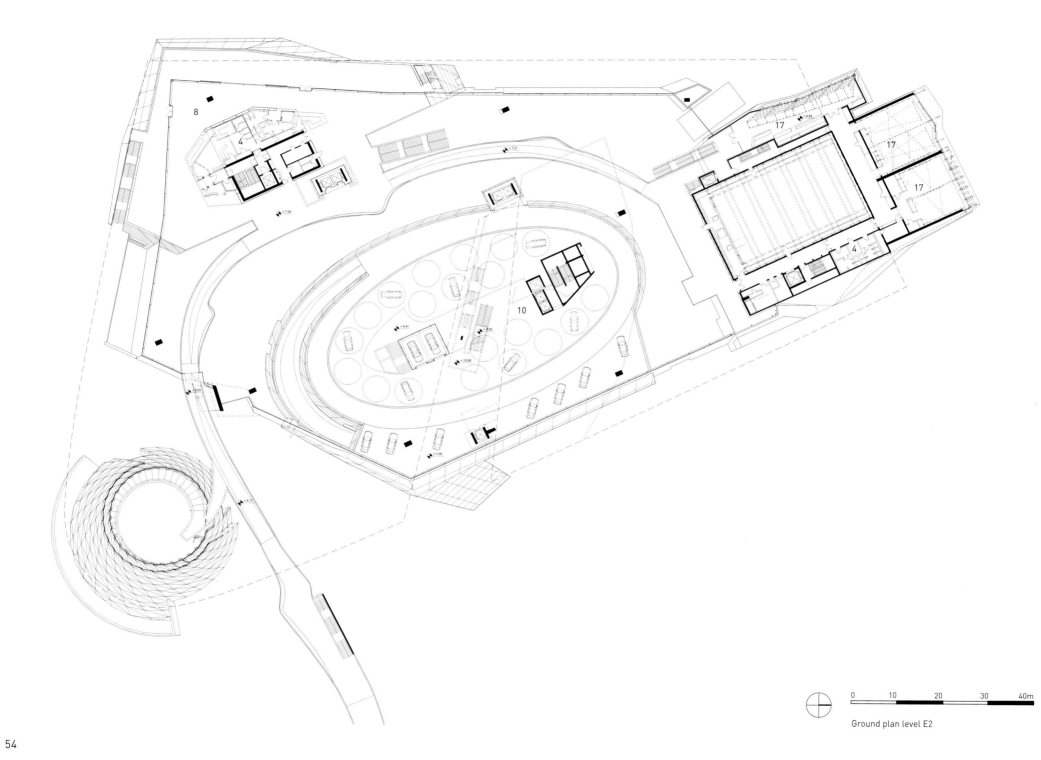

8

4

17   17   17

4

10

0   10   20   30   40m

Ground plan level E2

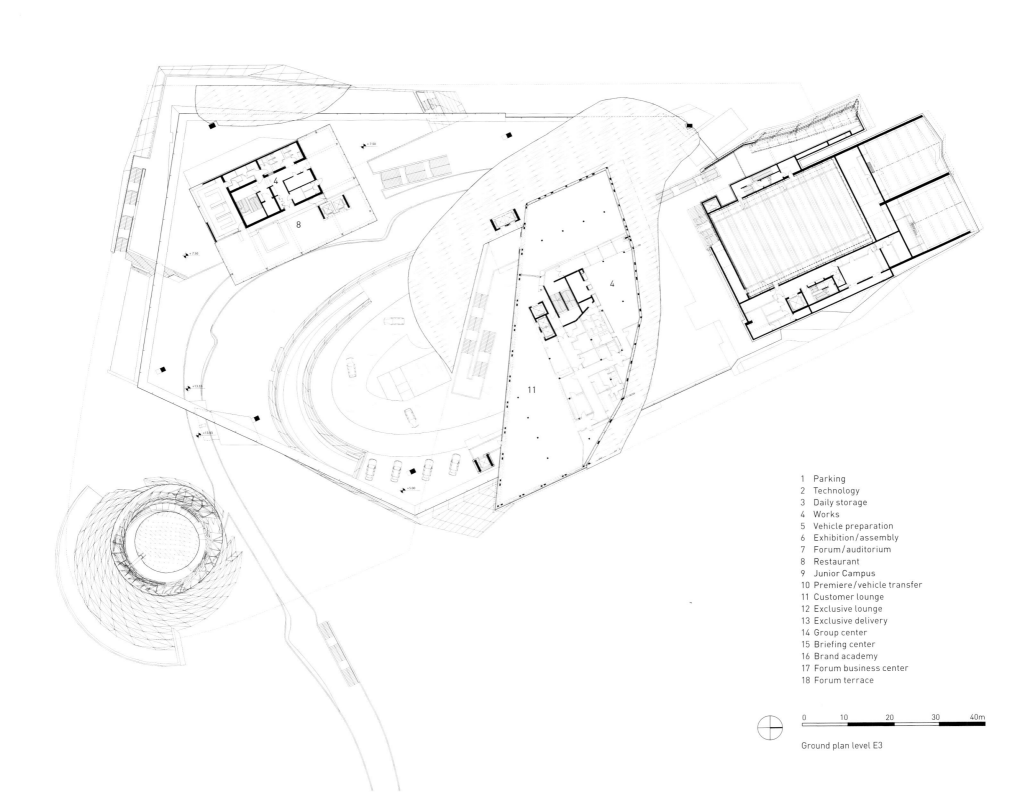

1 Parking
2 Technology
3 Daily storage
4 Works
5 Vehicle preparation
6 Exhibition/assembly
7 Forum/auditorium
8 Restaurant
9 Junior Campus
10 Premiere/vehicle transfer
11 Customer lounge
12 Exclusive lounge
13 Exclusive delivery
14 Group center
15 Briefing center
16 Brand academy
17 Forum business center
18 Forum terrace

0   10   20   30   40m

Ground plan level E3

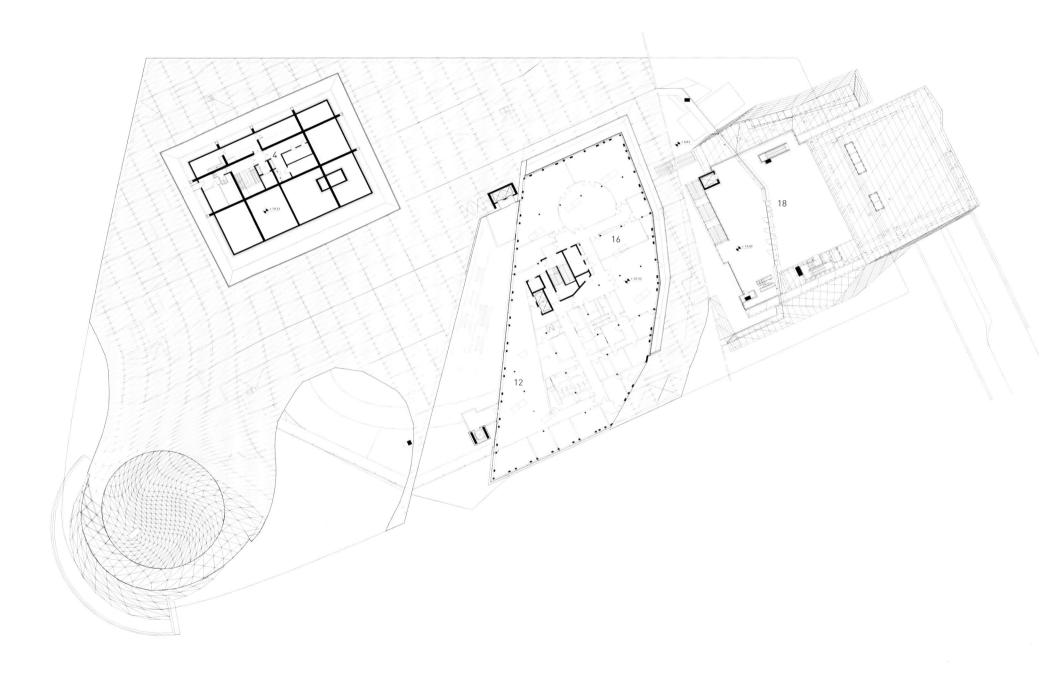

4

16

12

18

0   10   20   30   40m

Ground plan level E4

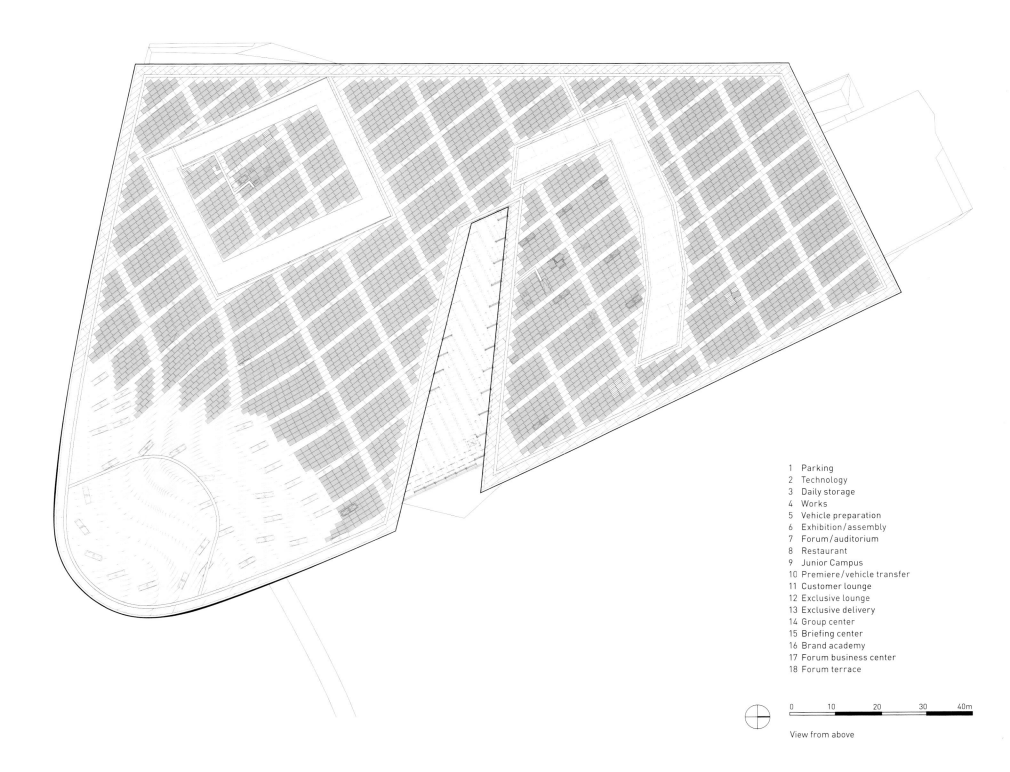

1 Parking
2 Technology
3 Daily storage
4 Works
5 Vehicle preparation
6 Exhibition/assembly
7 Forum/auditorium
8 Restaurant
9 Junior Campus
10 Premiere/vehicle transfer
11 Customer lounge
12 Exclusive lounge
13 Exclusive delivery
14 Group center
15 Briefing center
16 Brand academy
17 Forum business center
18 Forum terrace

0   10   20   30   40m

View from above

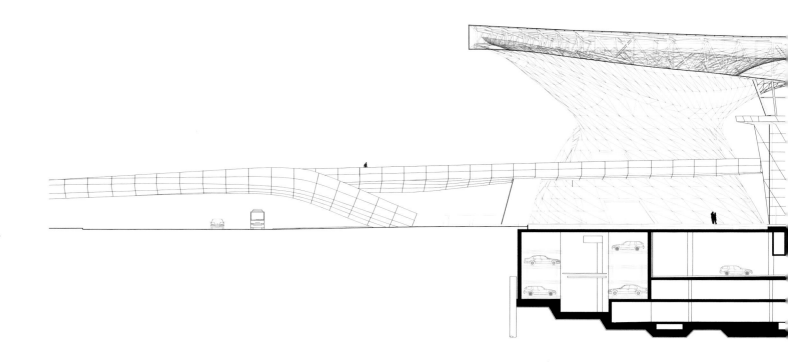

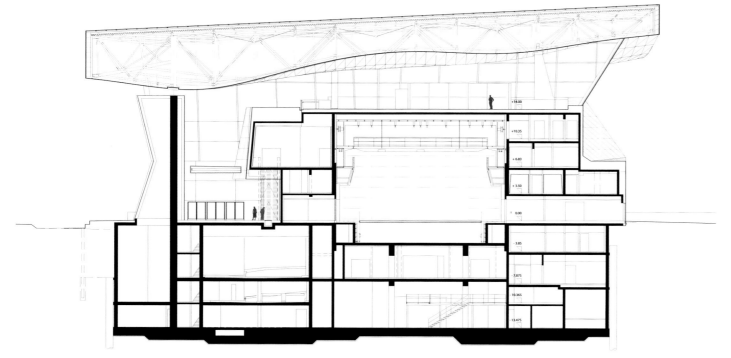

+14.00

+10.35

+6.83

+3.50

0.00

-3.85

-7.875

-10.365

-13.475

0 5 10 15 20 25m

Cross-section, Forum S14

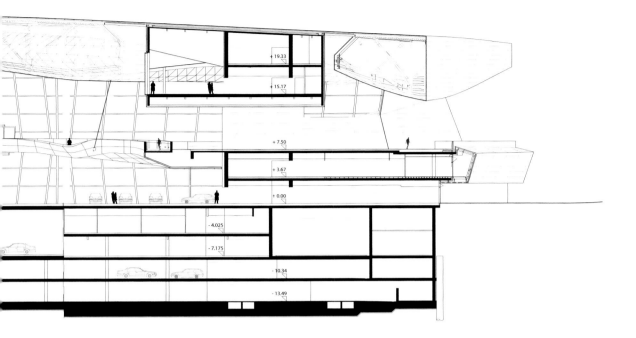

+ 19.33
+ 15.17
+ 7.50
+ 3.67
± 0.00
- 4.025
- 7.175
- 10.34
- 13.49

0   5   10   15   20   25m

Cross-section, Tower S3

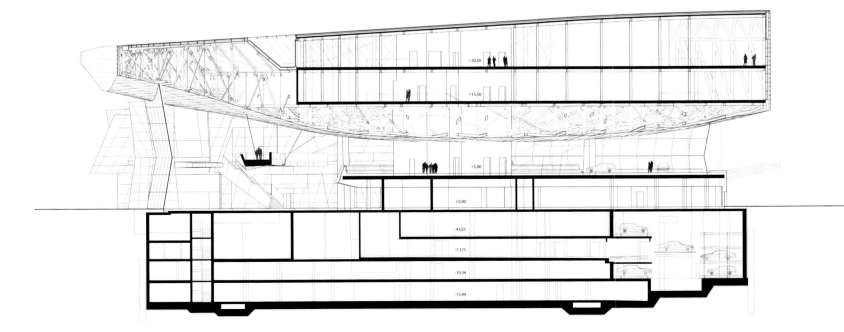

+ 20.50
+ 15.50
+ 5.00
± 0.00
- 4.025
- 7.175
- 10.34
- 13.49

0   5   10   15   20   25m

Cross-section, Lounge S4

59

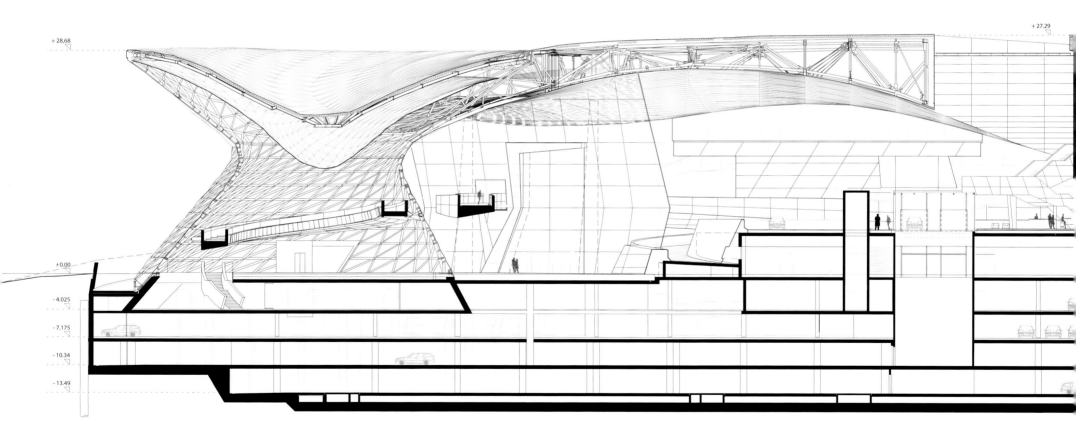

+ 28,68

+ 27,29

± 0.00

-4.025

-7.175

-10.34

-13.49

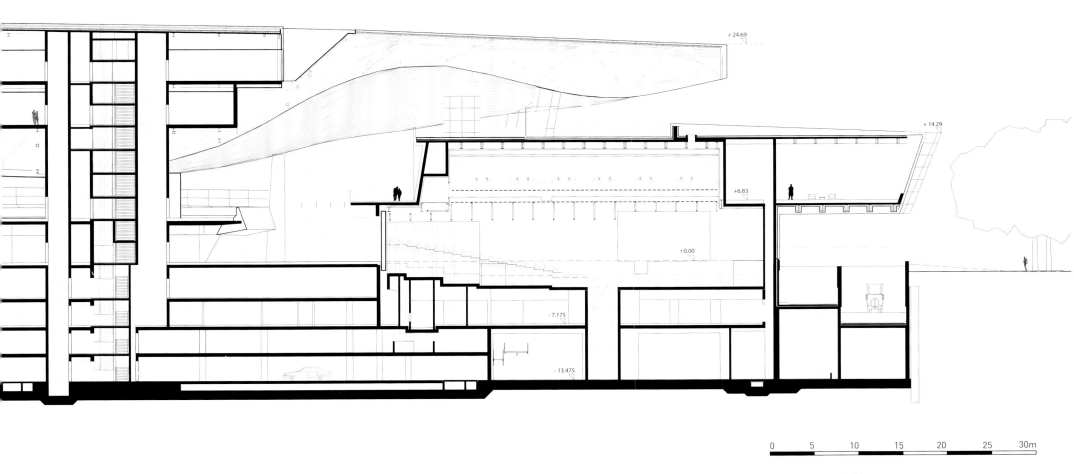

+ 24.69

+ 14.29

+6.83

±0.00

- 7.175

- 13.475

0   5   10   15   20   25   30m

Longitudinal section S1

Technology, Construction and Energy Design

The roof of BMW Welt takes on many control functions in respect of light, ventilation and acoustics. Traditional air-conditioning is used only in selected zones. Energy use is minimized.

Technology, construction and their interplay from the point of view of functional design and ecology were a focus from the very beginning of project development. A project like BMW Welt demands integrated planning at an early stage of development. The aspiration to develop form, function and their technical realization in parallel on the same high level led to hybrid concepts, which it was hoped would culminate in a fusion of low-tech and high-tech solutions. The requirements for the project were unusual. Vehicles were to drive through the Hall for delivery to customers while at the same time good air quality had to be preserved for the guests — and energy use kept to a minimum. In order to accomplish these feats, BMW Welt needed a "brain" in the form of computer systems. These systems perform at a capacity equivalent to 500 PCs. This is adequate because they have data links to BMW headquarters and can thus produce almost any information required.

The technical systems have a service function. Like an organism, they fulfill the tasks required for the special use of this building automatically, invisibly and silently. But within the scope of this environment, the technical systems not only fulfill this service function; they also ultimately lay the foundation for success. Despite this special and indispensable task, the "organism of a building" — i.e. its technical underpinning — does not evoke any emotions as a rule, and is simply taken for granted, unless of course the building technology for some reason fails in its task of keeping employees and visitors comfortable.

This building organism at BMW Welt encompasses all technical systems:

— Water supply networks for plumbing and fire extinguishing systems
— Sprinkler systems for automatic firefighting
— Cold and warm water networks for cooling and heating
— Air distribution networks for fresh air supply and waste air exhaust
— Extracting exhaust gases
— Automation networks to regulate/control the organism
— Distribution networks for electricity
— Safety networks for early detection of hazards
— Data networks for transmitting information.

Conception: The realization of the technical building facilities within the scope of the architecture led to a planning model with five thematic blocks: Hall, Premiere, Forum, Tower, Double Cone.

Hall

The technical solution here is based on previous experience with large halls. All of the necessary features were realized successfully according to a low-tech concept. The interrelations of daylight and artificial light with ambient climate and acoustics influence people's feeling of well-being in the Hall. The concept for the technological building systems takes up these relationships and integrates them in an interdependent manner, adapting their range of influence by modifying their dimensions or building in appropriate control mechanisms. A major goal in designing the systems was to save energy. This aim is achieved by minimizing the mechanical apparatus for ventilation, heating and cooling. The gigantic Hall is thus conceived as a solar-heated, naturally ventilated sub-climatic area, a multifunctional space that does not follow the otherwise customary requirements for heating and ventilation.

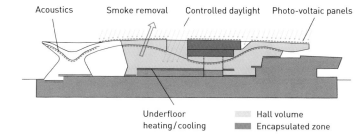

Acoustics   Smoke removal   Controlled daylight   Photo-voltaic panels

Underfloor heating/cooling   Hall volume   Encapsulated zone

A natural air supply is generated by thermal currents, wind pressure and turbulences when air accumulates in the area of the facade and roof projection. Air intake and outflow take place through automatically controlled vents. The "natural aeration" system provides sufficient fresh air to the Hall. The Hall's roof system has special significance for the complex made up of heat, cold and air. A 3D simulation of thermal currents and air streams was conducted in order to investigate the spread of exhaust fumes from the cars driven on the Premiere level. Iterative calculations were then carried out to optimize the arrangement of air intake and outflow vents for natural air exchange in such a way that it was possible to remain below the permitted threshold value of around ten percent. All of the requisite technical components, as well as fire prevention facilities, are located above the permeable stainless steel ceiling and cannot be seen from the Hall.

Premiere

The key task of the new BMW Welt is to deliver cars — in the Premiere section — with all concepts geared toward enhancing the experience of delivery. Because of the exhaust gases that this task involves, special considerations and calculations had to be made in terms of the ventilation plan, since the Premiere is open to the Hall — the major space in this world of experience. Beyond merely fine-tuning the volume of air intake and outflow currents, it was also important to extract the exhaust fumes directly and pump in fresh air. Planning here was based on an assumed turnover of 40 cars per hour, or 250 cars per day.

Appropriate air conditions for spending time and working in the Hall space are ensured by corresponding technical measures. The technical concept focused in particular on the specific demands placed on the room and function groups inserted into the Hall in their use as common rooms and/or permanent workplaces, including restaurants, kitchens, shops, design studios, lounges, offices, and social rooms.

Forum

The Forum is a separate event area for up to 1,200 persons, equipped to meet all the specifications for a full-fledged theater or conference room.

The ventilation technology fulfills the high demands on comfort and soundproofing placed on such a sensitive area when it is situated in the middle of other function areas. The technical facilities for this special area were conceived independently, including a plan for integrating them into the architecture. Air is supplied laterally via air jets and is extracted through the ceiling as exhaust air. Based on the number of people in the room, infinite adjustment of the required air volume is possible.

Tower

The technical equipment discreetly supports the gastronomic functions. In places where guests spend longer periods of time, air sources are placed near the floor. In order to ensure pleasant air quality even near the glass facades, the vertical facade support profiles are heated to prevent the cold downdrafts typical for this kind of construction.

Outflow vents for air exhaust are distributed throughout the space and centrally close to the kitchen section. This creates a graduated pressure gradient that prevents the spread of cooking

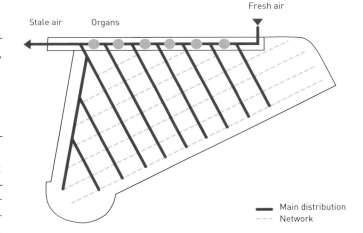

Stale air   Organs   Fresh air

——— Main distribution
- - - Network

odors, despite the fact that kitchen areas are open to, and visible from, the Hall. The guest zones are heated and cooled by means of floor heating and air conditioning, or by ceiling heating and cooling. In the kitchens cooled fresh air is brought in via large-surface air inlets. Exhaust air is extracted directly over the stoves. The resulting pressure gradient prevents outside air from flowing in.

Double Cone

The Double Cone is used as an exhibition space and for special events. Air is brought in by means of a low-induction system along the base of the facade and streams into the roof through the opening at the top of the cone. Floor air conditioning and air circulation coolers in the wall and floor areas ensure the necessary comfort level. In the in-between seasons, natural ventilation via facade shutters is used. The structural design of BMW Welt represents a special challenge when determining how to conduct supply lines. Because of the vast support-free space, which is borne by only 11 columns plus the elevator shafts, the supply cross-sections for the Lounge floors and the Tower had to be integrated into the few supporting core cross-sections. This situation necessitated close coordination at a very early project phase between those responsible for structural engineering, the routing of facility services and building technology.

Realization

Following the first technical simulations, it was possible to confirm that the selected solution was the right one and that no conventional climate control system was needed for the Hall. The volume of the Hall is much too large to ensure by means of conventional planning approaches the air exchange necessitated by the exhaust fumes of

the cars driving through it. The solution was to renounce large-scale mechanical and technical systems in favor of natural ventilation for the Hall. Air movements come about in a controlled manner by taking advantage of wind pressure and thermal currents in the Hall. Targeted extraction of exhaust gases prevents them from spreading and mixing with the ambient air. With this approach, the volume of the Hall could not be big enough. The underside of the roof is only an optical limit. It does not stop air currents from getting through.

Without large-channel ventilation systems, simply through the targeted utilization and intelligent control of air intake and outflow vents in connection with supplementary, likewise automatically controlled shade systems, it was possible to achieve a pleasant room climate throughout the year.

In the areas with permanent workplaces, such as the vehicle warehouse, the vehicle preparation area, the carwash, the vehicle handover area and the restaurants, "island solutions" were devised.

The complex technical systems were first reviewed and rated with respect to effectiveness. For this purpose, CFD (Computer Fluid Dynamics) calculations were carried out utilizing networked computing centers at the Technical University in Graz.

With the help of these methods, air currents and air distributions could be studied three-dimensionally under specific conditions or extreme conditions (heat waves, etc.) The same method was used to analyze the spread of vehicle emissions and to position the corresponding exhaust systems at the right points for ensuring air exchange.

The resulting system not only functions reliably; it is also efficient. Supplementary heating and cooling is conducted through the

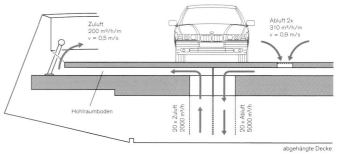

Technical data
Total volume flow rate: 420,000 m³/h
Air treatment zones: 20
Ventilation channels: 35,000 m²
Power output for heating: 3,600 kW
Power output for cooling: 2,700 kW
Total pipelines: 75,000 m
Sprinkler heads: 12,000
Water volume in sprinkler storage container: 1,400 m³
Pump output of sprinkler: 429 kW
Pump pressure: 9.6 bar
Delivery volume: 18,900 l/min
Hardware data points: 10,000
Software data points: 40,000

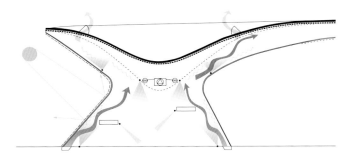

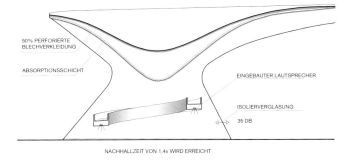

50% PERFORIERTE BLECHVERKLEIDUNG

ABSORPTIONSSCHICHT

EINGEBAUTER LAUTSPRECHER

ISOLIERVERGLASUNG

35 DB

NACHHALLZEIT VON 1,4s WIRD ERREICHT

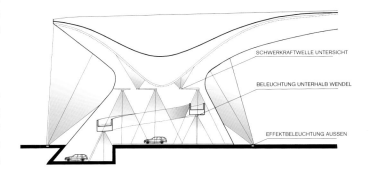

SCHWERKRAFTWELLE UNTERSICHT

BELEUCHTUNG UNTERHALB WENDEL

EFFEKTBELEUCHTUNG AUSSEN

Hall floor. The additional major interior heat loads — monitors, LED walls and stage lighting — were calculated with this method and alleviated with minimal energy expenditure.

The Organism

Along the western edge of the building, a services block that runs over levels –1 to –3 forms the backbone of the building's technical facilities. This building services "spine" is a stable axis for primary supply of the technical infrastructure. From here, comb-like projections under the ceiling of Level U0 form the primary supply network. All vertical conduits and the supply grid branch off from this horizontal comb structure — with the sector channels connected through the floor on Level 0. The services block can be accessed on Level U1 from the supply road. Thus, it is possible to walk into all central areas from the supply road in order to transport devices in and out without problem.

All the ventilation equipment is arranged along this spine, including the central air conduction and distribution systems with the corresponding treatment units. The "arteries" of the organism are the supply and disposal conduits for electricity, data, water, heat, cold and air branching off from the spine. The "network" is a system of sector channels or access points that allow for flexible responses to changing demands. This makes it possible for BMW Welt to host a variety of functions and events. This system corresponds to the trade-show standard for a supply and disposal grid with media support points. Media support points consist of shafts with cover plates that are removable and can be driven over, in order to convey temporary fixtures in and out of the Hall.

Solar Power System

The idea of integrating the engineering and technical systems into the functional sculpture of BMW Welt while calling into question traditional solutions was likewise consistently pursued when integrating a solar power system in the roof membrane. Since the view onto the roof of BMW Welt as the fifth facade plays just as important a role in the communicative impact of the building's outer skin as the four walls, a traditional fan-like raised arrangement of solar cells facing south was out of the question.

In conventional systems the output of south-facing cells in a reference year was about 16% higher than that of cells that were placed horizontally. However, the choice of special high-quality black glass-foil solar panels helped to almost balance out this difference. By avoiding mutual shadows cast between the cells in winter, it was additionally possible to reduce the lost energy production caused by snow cover in comparison to a standard solution. The installed solar power system has a nominal output of 810 kWp with 3,660 solar panels and an area of approx. 8,000 square meters. The solar panels were integrated flush with the surface of a stainless steel cover that fits over the actual roof drainage level. In this way, visible penetrations through the roof and visible exhaust structures were avoided.

Wind Simulation/Wind Tunnel

The complex geometry of the outer skin of the building calls into question the accepted norms derived from conventional building geometries. On the other hand, these complex geometries can serve to strengthen both positive and negative effects. In order to be able to estimate these effects as a basis for planning, and to generate guideline pressure values for structural engineering calculations, CD analyses were used to examine the effect the outer skin has on wind currents. Twelve different windstream directions with different speeds were evaluated. The results showed that the currently valid regulations could not be applied to the Double Cone with its special geometry and placement in the structure. It had substantially higher suction and pressure peaks than a comparable cylinder. Due to the serious implications of this data, the results of the computer simulation were verified and confirmed using wind tunnel tests.

Artificial Light and Daylight

Daylight is characterized by constant changes in light quantity and quality; it changes with the weather, time of day and time of year. In addition to the amount of light, the direction, color and spectral composition of the light and the relationship between diffuse and directed light are subject to constant fluctuations. This continual change on the one hand constitutes the problem in using daylight to illuminate a high-quality interior, but on the other hand provides the high quality that is expected and demanded from a daylight source in psychological terms. In the course of the planning process, the specific requirements placed on the building by the various functions posed special challenges to the planning of artificial light and daylight.

While a high degree of transparency and daylight were desired in BMW Welt, at the same time the glass and high-gloss painted surfaces of the cars reflect every source of light and leave no room for error. Contrasts that are too stark, as might happen with direct daylight in a building, distort the forms of the vehicles. The materiality in the interplay between artificial light and daylight therefore

has considerable significance. The amount of daylight entering the building on days of varying sunshine had to be harmonized as much as possible with the lighting situation under cloudy skies. By lighting up the underside of the ceiling, a diffuse ambient light is created. The sunlight shining directly through facades or roof openings was reduced using moveable (anti-glare roller blinds) and rigid sun-shading measures (projecting roof surfaces, perforated metal facades) to the extent that no large-scale disruptions were possible, while preserving the perception from within the building of the daily course of the sun and, even on sunny days, ensuring that the view toward the outside was largely maintained. Since the distribution of light density in the clear sky changes greatly with the position of the sun, the distribution of daylight within the building at any time can only be determined when the sun's position is known. The strength of illumination created by direct sunlight is so high in almost the entire course of the year and of the day that it would lead to too much glare and also generate considerable heat in the interior. Shading is thus required for most functions.

To assess the direct sunlight, a 1:200 model of the building design formed the basis for a laboratory test using an artificial, moveable sun and video recordings made with endoscopic cameras. The goal was to precisely specify the impact of direct sunlight on the main exhibition areas (Premiere) of the building and to check the effect of skylight openings in interaction with the facades. In the further stages of daylight planning the findings from these model investigations were optimized in relation to glare protection and blackout systems.

The decision on what materials to deploy, particularly for the Hall with its areas for vehicle presentation, was essential to the desired

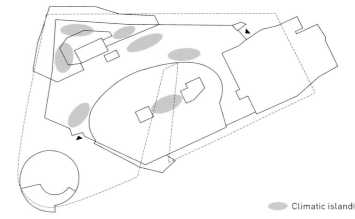

Climatic island

Concept for the ventilation of the hall (preliminary design stage)

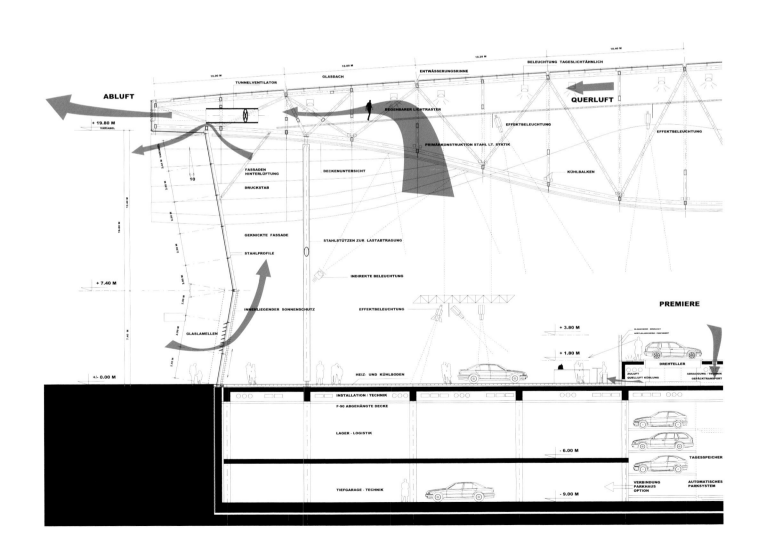

ABLUFT

QUERLUFT

TUNNELVENTILATOR

GLASDACH

ENTWÄSSERUNGSRINNE

BELEUCHTUNG TAGESLICHTÄHNLICH

+ 19.80 M
VARIABEL

BEGEHBARER LICHTRASTER

EFFEKTBELEUCHTUNG

EFFEKTBELEUCHTUNG

PRIMÄRKONSTRUKTION STAHL LT. STATIK

FASSADEN
HINTERLÜFTUNG

DECKENUNTERSICHT

KÜHLBALKEN

10

DRUCKSTAB

GEKNICKTE FASSADE

STAHLSTÜTZEN ZUR LASTABTRAGUNG

STAHLPROFILE

+ 7.40 M

INDIREKTE BELEUCHTUNG

PREMIERE

INNENLIEGENDER SONNENSCHUTZ

EFFEKTBELEUCHTUNG

+ 3.80 M

+ 1.80 M

GLASLAMELLEN

DREHTELLER

+/- 0.00 M

HEIZ- UND KÜHLBODEN

ZULUFT
QUELLUFT KÜHLUNG

ABSAUGUNG / TECHNIK
GEPÄCKTRANSPORT

INSTALLATION / TECHNIK

F-90 ABGEHÄNGTE DECKE

LAGER - LOGISTIK

- 6.00 M

TAGESSPEICHER

VERBINDUNG
PARKHAUS
OPTION

AUTOMATISCHES
PARKSYSTEM

TIEFGARAGE - TECHNIK

- 9.00 M

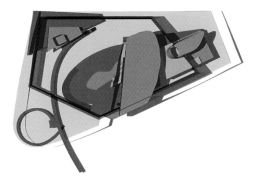

Shading study according to position of sun in July and December
Below: Daylight study to investigate light incidence using a 1:200 scale model

effect. The surfaces were on the one hand to reflect the light as diffusely as possible, but also to take up the light in all its variations and reflect it as naturally as possible.

Glass-bead-blasted stainless steel was ultimately chosen as the ideal material for the surfaces of the roof and facades. Using various blasting materials and grains, it was possible to achieve the desired matte reflective effect. All building parts, with the exception of structural elements such as columns and facade posts, were clad in this material. Some 42,000 square meters were used. The material and surface of the Hall floor also had to be coordinated with the lighting since a bright reflection onto the metal surface of the underside of the roof was to be achieved.

The light within the building not only fulfills a functional task but also harbors an emotional component. The idea is to convey the image of a cloud. This image serves as the guiding principle of the design. It thus seemed only natural to allude to this metaphor in the building's lighting as well: the cloud as a dynamic element embodying all variants and varieties of light. Diffuse, flat light, combined with openings that let in rays of accented light generate a dynamic and suspense-filled atmosphere in the building. Bearing in mind the flexibility of the tasks and the various spatial functions in the building, the lighting must be able to react to almost anything, anywhere.

The underside of a cloud never has a uniform, homogenous color or surface — it "lives." Broad-surface light produced by a component with multiple lighting options, accentuated with narrow rays of light from the underside of the "cloud," similar to rays of sunlight, and combined with an adjustable color component, yields an overall scene that supports the desired emotions and functions. In interac-

tion with the roofing material, the "cloud" can be experienced as both a volume and as a lightweight, dynamic element.

In addition to its effect by night, with the help of artificial light the conspicuous Double Cone must serve the same function by day. In model studies performed with an artificial sun we observed that the Double Cone captures the direct rays of the sun and thus presents itself as a body by day, unfolding an impact on the overall building. In order to realize this effect and at the same time ensure sun and glare protection, the entire portion of the Double Cone that is exposed to the sun was shaded by a second skin of perforated stainless steel. This sun protection acts as a diffuser and can both keep direct sunlight from falling into the interior and also "capture" it and make the cone glow, making it look like a body from outside by day while it conversely glows from within at night.

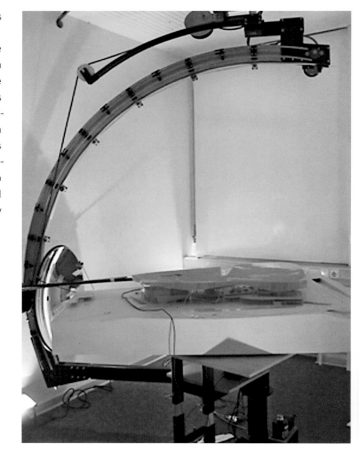

68

Fire Prevention

BMW Welt falls under the section for special buildings in the Bavarian Building Code. The diverse heterogeneous usages made it necessary to combine the regulations in several different sets of rules. By merging these requirements as well as taking advantage of relief provisions for points of sale and places of assembly, as well as other regulations, the required multifunctionality was ensured.

The roof of BMW Welt spans an area of approx. 18,000 square meters. It was essential to the design that this area should not and could not be divided by firewalls. This situation was exacerbated by the fact that the vertical staggering of functions also made open connections over several stories necessary. The law allows a maximum fire compartment size of 5,000 square meters per floor. The base area of the Hall is around 13,000 square meters on the ground floor alone. In order not to have to work here with complicated technical solutions or even physical firewalls, the concept of the air firewall was introduced; without visible structural measures, this ensures that the maximum fire compartment sizes are maintained. The air firewall forms a 10-meter-wide swath straight through BMW Welt, also functioning as a necessary escape route. The use of this area for presentations is restricted. Because of the spatial complexity of the structure, the air firewall had to be slanted in the area of the Lounge in order to comply with the fire prevention regulations.

Building sections such as the Forum, Tower, Lounge and Double Cone are treated as independent structures in terms of fire prevention. Due to the large volume of the Hall, it was very easy to demonstrate that there were smoke-free layers to make the rescue routes secure. The technical components for fire prevention include a sprinkler system throughout the building, an automatic fire-alarm system and special additions such as permanent redundant oxygen reduction in the short-term storage tanks to prevent incipient fires.

It was possible to permanently reduce the oxygen ratio in the short-term storage tanks from 21 to 15 percent. Thus no additional stairwells had to be built to ensure access to the short-term storage tanks by the fire department in case of fire. This was fortunate, since the stairwells would have conflicted with building use, especially on the ground floor.

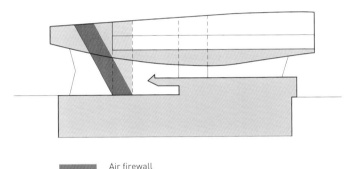

Air firewall

Excavation pit with tension piles for buoyancy control, summer 2004

1

Double Cone

The Double Cone is a central element of the design of BMW Welt. It visualizes the soaring dynamics of the building with its continuous transition into the seemingly floating roof. The Double Cone takes the form of two leaning truncated cones with a rounded transition between them. In structural engineering terms, it is conceived as a framework shell made of horizontal rings and two ascending diagonal bands. Both bands are spiral-shaped and turn in the same direction in order to further enhance the impression of dynamism. The mesh size of the Double Cone was originally oriented to that of the roof grid. The glazing was done by means of a secondary structure. The Double Cone is a main roof support element and also plays an essential role in horizontal reinforcement since the horizontal loads in the solid building structure below the Double Cone are discharged via its base points.

Due to the special proposal mentioned at the beginning, the mesh size was halved in order to match that of the glass panes and slide the triangular panes directly into the rectangular hollow profiles measuring 300 x 100 millimeters or 250 x 100 millimeters. In order to ensure the necessary support, all joints were welded into an unbending skeleton shell. The Double Cone is closed on top by a suspended roof with radial and tangential girders, which is hung in a bend-resistant ring-shaped three-chord support. Special challenges to planning, logistics and the construction workflow were posed by technical systems such as control lines, sprinkler systems, power supply, and heating and cooling systems integrated into the supporting profiles of the Double Cone shell. Since the load-bearing cross-sections could not be weakened in any way, systems had to be pre-installed and stainless steel used for the sprinkler pipes to protect against corrosion.

Since the Double Cone and the entire roof including all supporting components work together as a complex complete system, studies of the load-bearing behavior of the various elements and the requisite proofs had to be carried out on the system as a whole. As already described in the "Roof" section, the Double Cone and the roof structure with all of the load-transfer components were represented in a complete model at an early stage. This allowed the effects of the planning updates on individual components to be directly monitored on the overall system and transferred to a 3D model.

Two basic procedures had to be mastered in the structural assembly: firstly the actual erection of the Double Cone structure out of individual components (constructing the cone structure, putting on the ring support, hanging the trusses in the interim area), and secondly coupling with the main roof and the ensuing load-transfer scenarios.

The successive construction of the grid elements was done using auxiliary structures and supporting scaffolding. After these components were in place, the ring supports, broken down into transportable parts, were set onto an encircling scaffolding, aligned and screwed in or welded. Then the intermediate beams were added according to plan (subordinate to the assembly of the suspended roof structure).

In order to achieve a controlled lowering of the entire roof structure, spindles were specified for the ring girders. Since no major shifts in force could be allowed, either from the main support structure to the Double Cone or vice-versa, a corresponding plan had to be developed for safely lowering the roof. The triangular glass panes were protected from pressure by means of sealing profiles resting directly on the hollow steel profiles, held in place at punctiform joints to shield them against the forces of suction or lifting. Finite element models were used to calculate these forces, based on the TRLV (Technical Directives for Linearly Mounted Glazing).

Development of the roof
The roof form was generated by superimposing the functional zones,
structurally necessary support heights, and by visualizing dynamic forces.

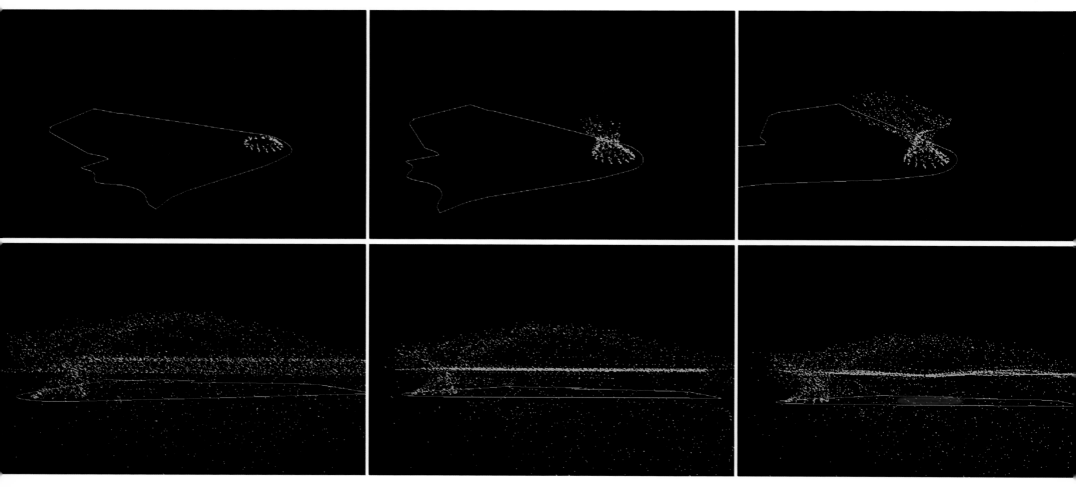

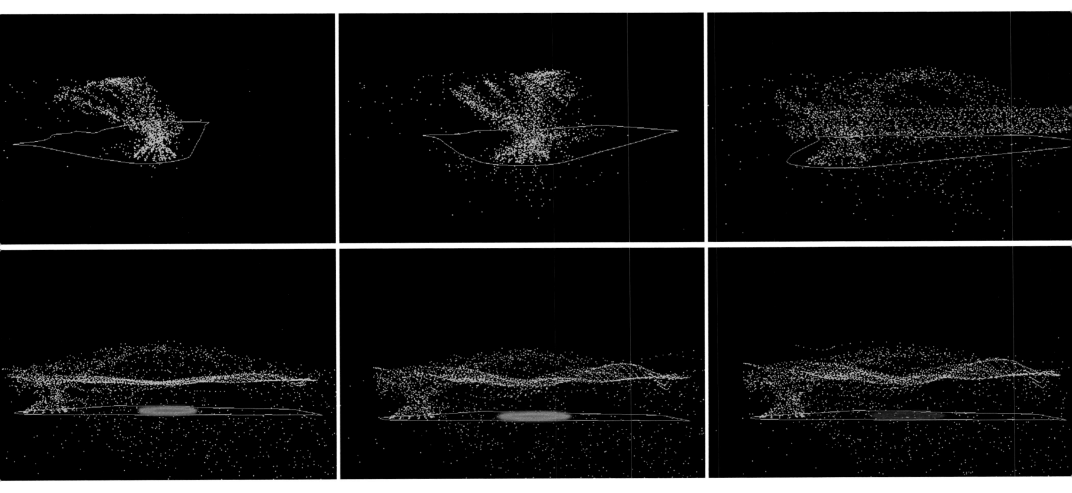

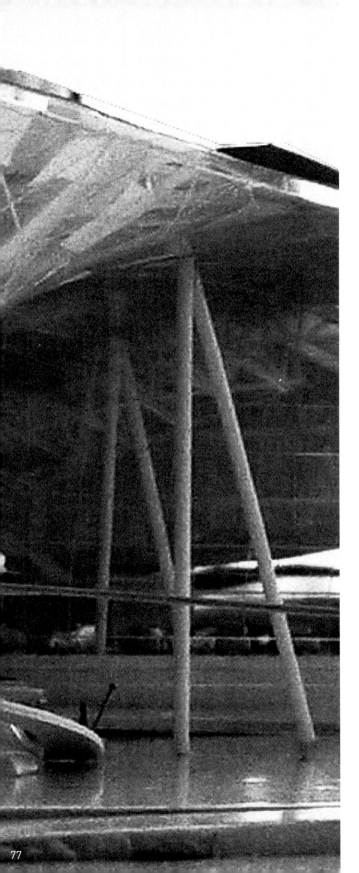

Flow of forces from the roof into the Double Cone
Concept for taking the weight of the roof in the area of the Double Cone. The cone is both a vertical load-bearing element and responsible for horizontal rigidity.

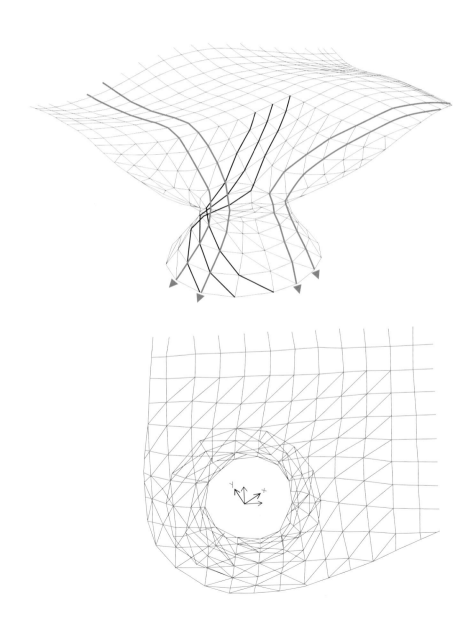

Structure of the Double Cone steel construction, design
Below: Structure of the Double Cone, special proposal with
annular bearing structure and suspended basket

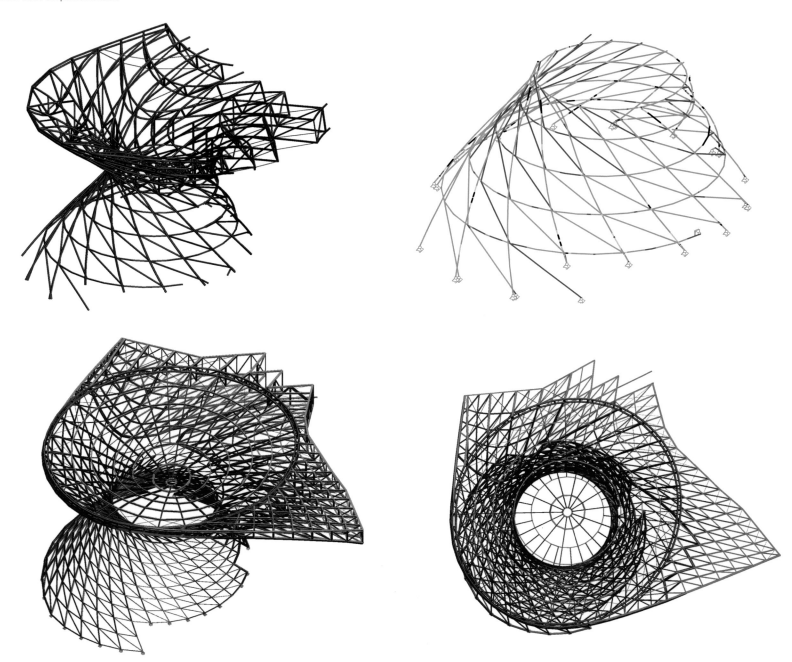

01.04.2005

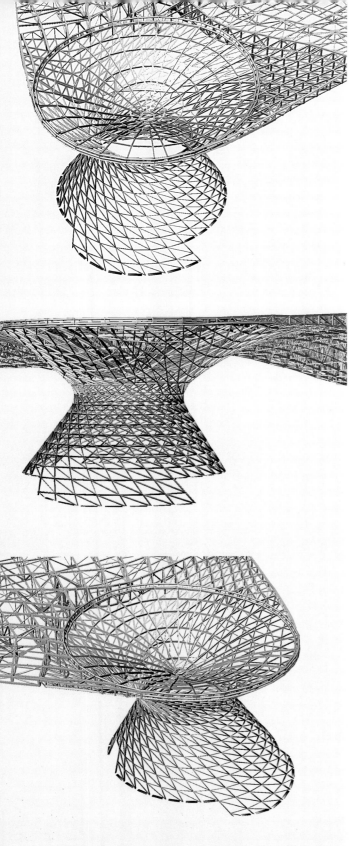

Axonometric depiction of the steel construction as executed; for fire safety reasons, the lower part of the Double Cone was given an F-30 coating.

26.01.2006

Cross-section of the Double Cone, section 1

Right: Aerial photograph of the building crane for the Double Cone during construction. In contrast to the original plan, the roof support structure connects up with a three-part ring support system.

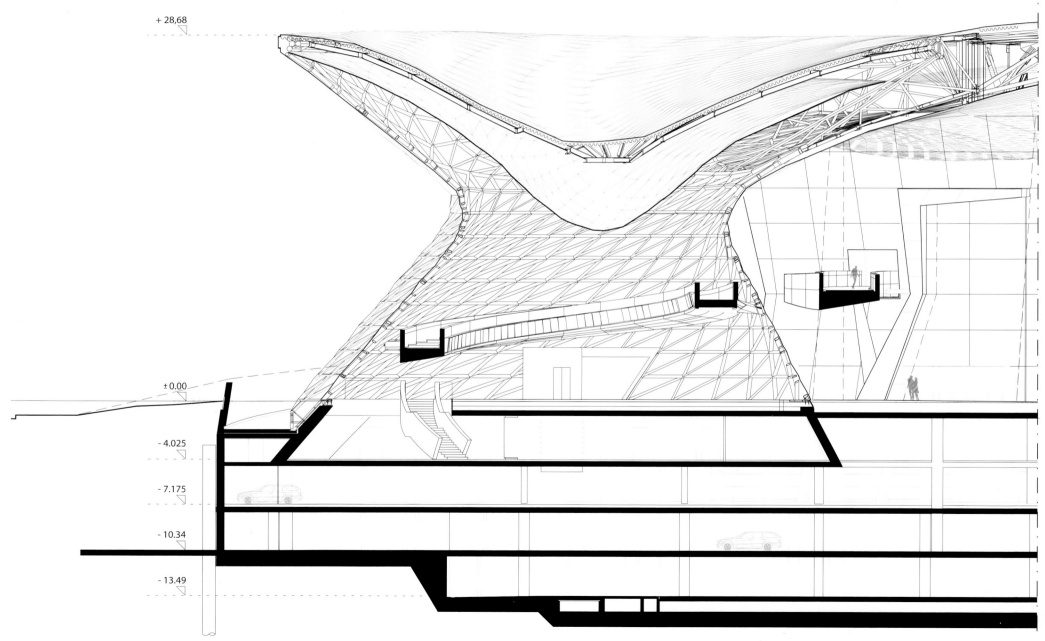

+ 28,68

± 0.00

- 4.025

- 7.175

- 10.34

- 13.49

09.09.2005

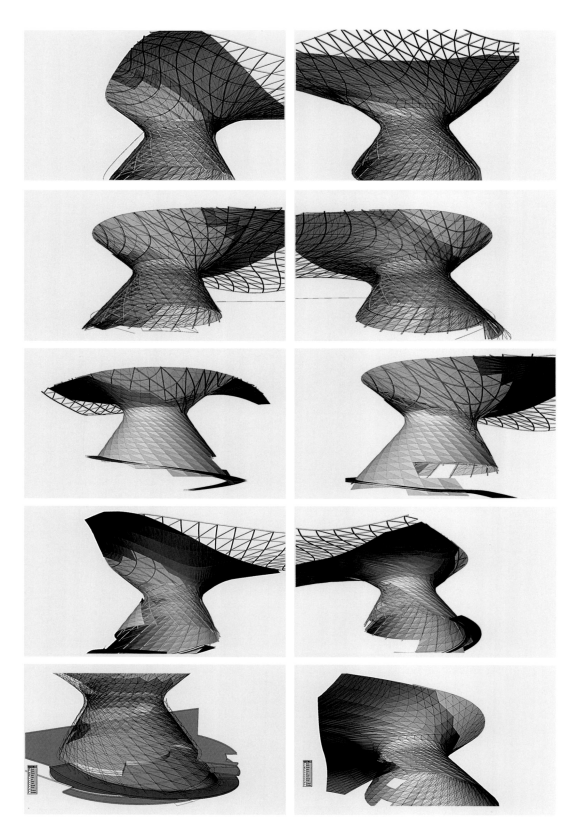

Axonometric depiction of the glazing of the Double Cone and the steel cladding

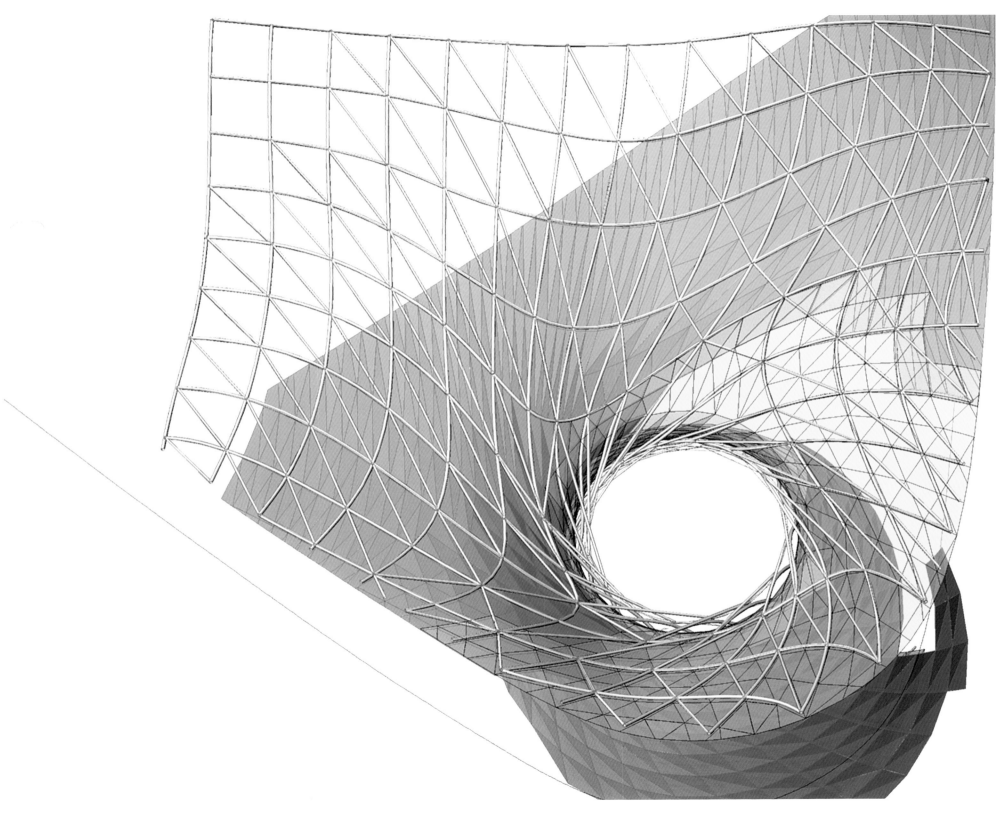

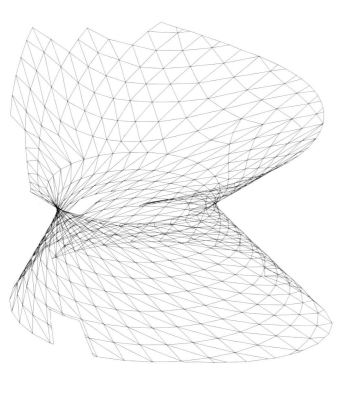

Left: Axonometric depiction of the glass surfaces of the Double Cone
The steel construction had always to be oriented axially to the facetted
outer structure. This leads to complex spatial overlaps of the individual
steel profile elements in the nodes.
Right: View of the Double Cone with SHEV slipstream openings
Below: Development of the glass surfaces in the Double Cone

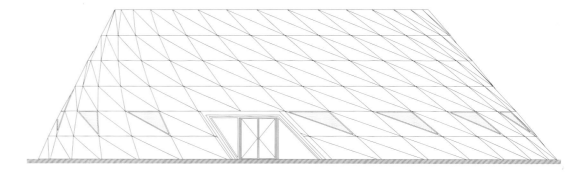

13.10.2006

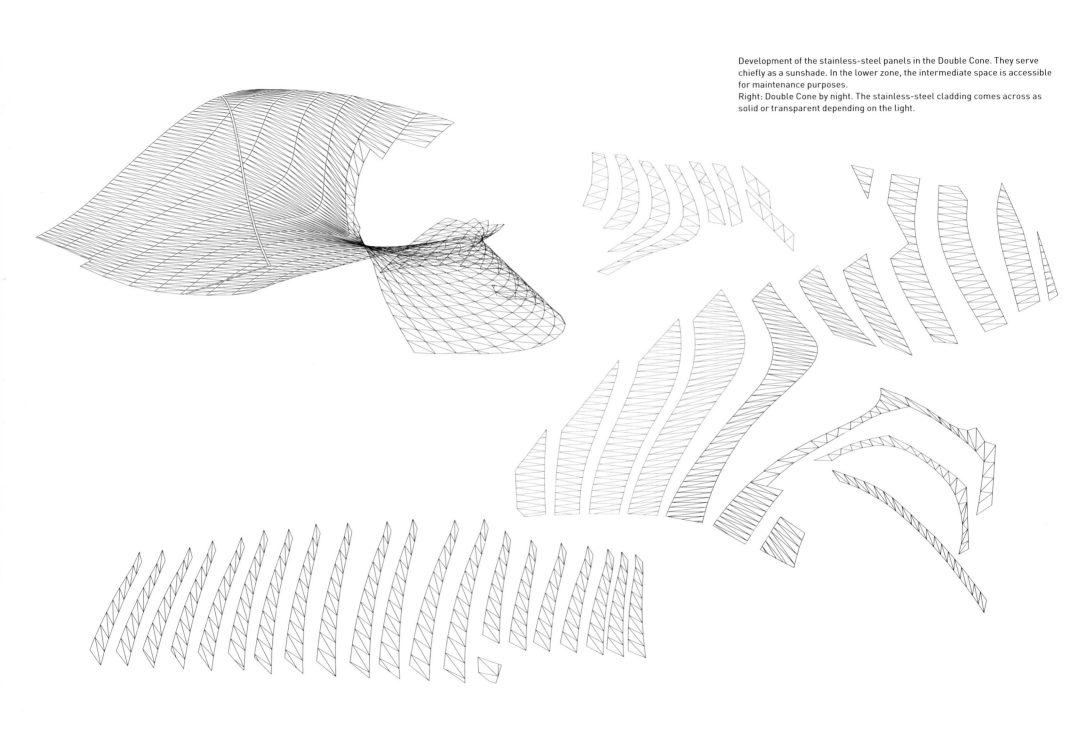

Development of the stainless-steel panels in the Double Cone. They serve chiefly as a sunshade. In the lower zone, the intermediate space is accessible for maintenance purposes.
Right: Double Cone by night. The stainless-steel cladding comes across as solid or transparent depending on the light.

17.07.2007

Reflected ceiling plan and axonometric view of the suspended stainless-steel ceiling

Right: Interior of the Double Cone with gravity wave; the latter has a major influence on the acoustic characteristics.

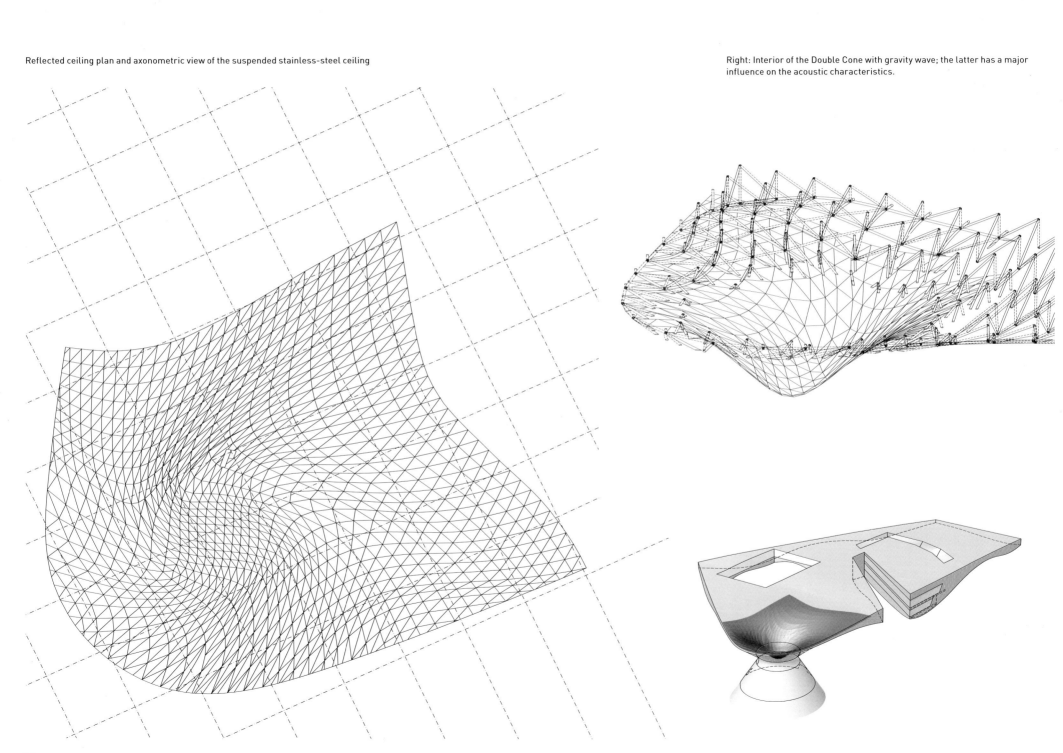

03.09.2007

95

19.10.2006

The helical ramp is suspended from consoles linked to the steel bearing structure of the Double Cone. The ramp is designed as a torsion carrier, so that only vertical forces are taken by the cone exterior.

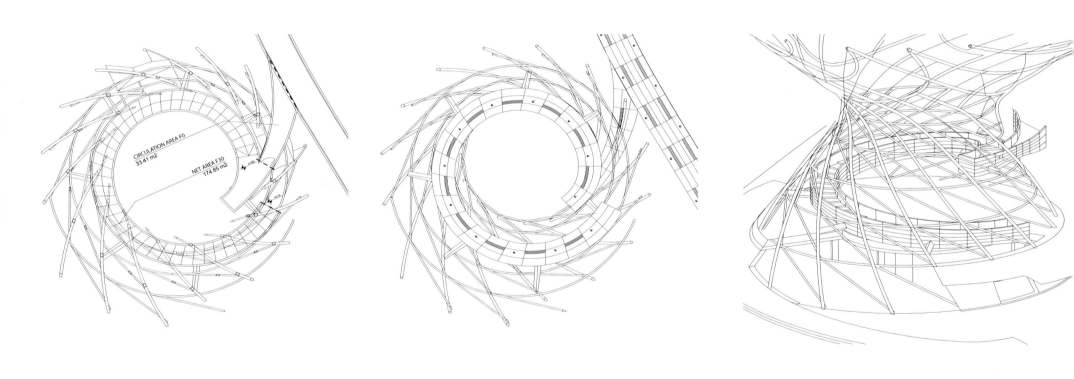

CIRCULATION AREA F0
33.41 m2

NET AREA F30
174.85 m2

16.03.2007

Structure of the steel construction, helical ramp,
designed as a torsion-rigid cross-section

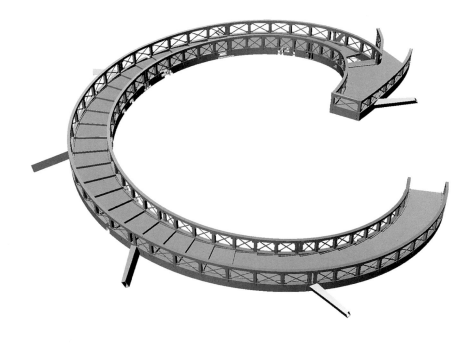

99

15.10.2005

04.09.2007

04.09.2007

04.09.2007

2

Roof

The roof is an upper stage for changing events as well as a space-differentiating sculpture that subdivides the space into various rooms. Unlike conventional architectural designs, the roof of BMW Welt not only forms the space-enclosing upper limit of the building, but also forms in conjunction with the Double Cone a functional, structural and above all formally independent structure. The support structure is an integral component of the building's architecture. Its development was thus also a component of the design process. Studies for planning the support structure already fulfilled two tasks during the various phases of the competition: first, the "obligatory" demonstration of the feasibility of the targeted architectural solution, and second — almost as in a "freestyle event" — they served to back up and steer the design process as well as to strengthen the architectural approach. Keywords here are lightness and floating, a playful handling of the visual impression of gravitation and of our visual habits.

The roof was designed in parallel to the iteratively overlapping processes. The development was carried out on the basis of working models, which were immediately digitized in a parallel process. The results and findings of this process were then in turn incorporated back into the model for formal inspection. The parallel process of planning the support structure was done using a framework program. Firstly two even, bendable girder grid layers with a grid size of 5.0 x 5.0 meters were deformed by fictitious load scenarios. The upper girder grid was cambered upward like a cushion through its own negative weight, and forces were exerted on the lower one conducted from the surfaces and building structures underneath it.

The resulting forms were monitored and optimized in respect of the meaningfulness of the load transfer. The various heights of the support structure elements are adapted to the stresses they must withstand. The interplay of the two girder layers as spatial support structure emerged from the addition of diagonal truss braces. To equalize the stress on the nodes and reduce the free lengths of the top and bottom chords, the points connecting the diagonals of the crossing truss braces are arranged in a staggered pattern. This yielded a lightweight and efficient support structure which, despite the vast expanses to be spanned, could be realized with relatively low material requirements. The vertical support of the roof was effected in the competition design by a series of circulating A-shaped supports, arranged eight meters from the outer edge of the roof and set toward the inside. Further support was provided by the Double Cone and the Lounge, which is conceived as an independent structure. In order to enhance the impression of floating, these circulating supports were then omitted when the program was consolidated in the subsequent design process. Instead, the structural components that were part of the design anyway were utilized as load-bearing elements without effecting the efficiency of the support structure, with just a few additional columns required.

Following the competition, as well as in the course of execution planning, a phase of intensive collaboration began for the architects and engineers as well as the planning team, both internally as well as with the contractors, who were chosen for their fabrication and assembly expertise in steel construction. The contractors made various special proposals by which the design was specified in greater detail, developed and modified. The aim was to do justice to the variety of different uses on the various floors with their wide range of special requirements — keeping these in mind on the construction site, in the construction process and in the ongoing construction and assembly conditions. The extra challenge from the point of view of planning the support structure was not only the complexity of the geometries and of the resulting support systems and models; it was also necessary, for example, to illustrate the roof construction with all of the load transfer components in an overall model. This in certain cases not only prompted changes in the design of the directly affected component, but also led to wider-reaching modifications of the entire system. For example, if in the course of planning there were significant changes to the rigidity of a reinforcing core, this could lead to shifts in the stresses that affected the entire roof structure, necessitating recalculations of the complete system. The overall planning thus took the form of an iterative process that could only be accomplished through the closest cooperation between all those involved as well as through clearly defined interfaces for exchanging data. Both architects and engineers continuously updated a 3D model to reflect the ongoing changes. The constant reconciliation of the models was essential to the design phase.

A significant example of the modifications and optimizations made during the design phase can be seen in the ongoing development of the roof structure. While in the competition design the roof was supported by a circulating series of reverse-V supports, the planning team aspired to reduce the number of supports in order to further enhance the floating impression made by the cloud-like roof. All supports were removed from the calculation model and, in addition to the remaining support afforded by the Double Cone and the Lounge, the roof was then coupled with the steel-reinforced concrete structure of the massive cores making up the Tower, Lounge and Forum areas. Where it was unavoidable for structural

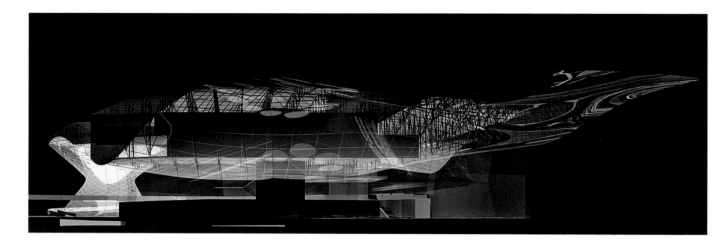

Perforated stainless steel sheeting was used for the underside of the roof, creating a variety of different moods depending on the use of lighting.
Below: Studies for the slope of the roof membrane and the curvature of the underside

engineering reasons, new supports were introduced, taking into consideration the architectural limiting conditions.

The basic concept of the roof support structure still consisted of two spatially distorted girder grid layers, which, with the addition of diagonal trusses in both axis directions and vertical posts at selected points, form a spatial support structure. To reduce stress on the nodes and reduce the free lengths of the top and bottom chords, the points connecting the diagonals of the crossing truss braces are arranged in a staggered pattern. In the areas where, due to varying spans or indirect support, the orthogonally arranged lattice girders could not be inter-hung relying only on the bending strength of the top and bottom chords, vertical connecting beams were introduced.

In the regular roof area, it was possible to arrange the top chords in a polygonal pattern and to bend the bottom chords uni-directionally. In the area of the Double Cone, the top and bottom chords were bent bi-directionally, which was effected by the axial skewing of uni-directionally bent pipes against one another. The Double Cone, which takes the form of two eccentric truncated cones, was made of horizontal rings, 16 bi-directionally bent ascending profiles and diagonals. The mesh size of the Double Cone is oriented to that of the roof grid. The glass facade was at first planned as a second layer.

In the transitional area between roof and Double Cone, the bending support system of the roof structure changes into a shell-like support effect in the Double Cone. For the top and bottom chords as well as the profiles of the Double Cone, pipes were planned that measured 323.9 millimeters in diameter, with varying wall thicknesses. The diagonals of the roof support structure were to be realized as well using round pipes with a regular diameter of 244 millimeters. The horizontal reinforcement of the roof was to be ensured

for one thing by the Double Cone structure, into the pliable base points of which the horizontal loads resulting from the solid building underneath the Double Cone had to be conducted. The steel-reinforced concrete structures of the Tower, Lounge and Forum are also activated as bracing cores by means of horizontal links with the roof support structure, conveying the resulting stresses into the ground.

The entire structure of the roof and Double Cone was modeled as a three-dimensional skeleton frame construction, taking into account at the end nodes of the members the degree of freedom in the respective connecting or support joints. The elasticity of the cross-sections was demonstrated, and local and global stability examined using the approach of suitable equivalent imperfections in the overall system and calculations based on second-order theory. The cores were modeled with their actual rigidity in order to maintain the distribution of internal force variables for the transfer of loads in the solid structure. Various borderline states of the overall system were taken into consideration here: the core being examined for load transfer in each case was assumed as uncracked, while for the rigidity of the remaining cores State II was assumed.

In conjunction with the contractor companies, special proposals for the Double Cone and regular roof were made to further reduce steel consumption. The consistent design of the structure using bent pipes would have required elaborate connections between the pipes, however, which would have had to be welded on site for the most part. With the huge dimensions, including up to 15 meters lattice height and the free-form design of the spatial lattice, prefabrication would hardly have been possible. The practical implementation of the special proposals made for the roof and Double Cone

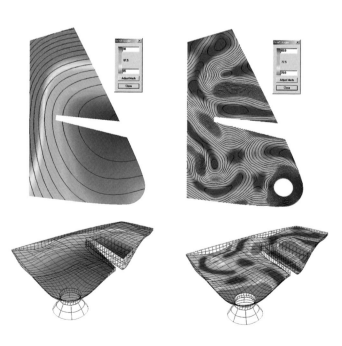

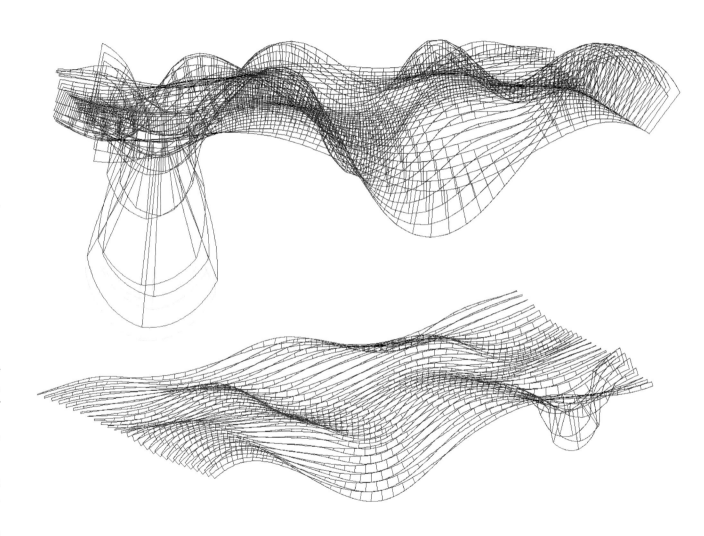

Gaussian analysis of the underside of the roof

aimed at a systematic simplification of the system with regard to more economical fabrication and a rapid assembly process. The following main steps were followed here: The initial system proposed in the original design of the support structure was a spatial lattice girder system, irregular in some sections, made out of pipe profiles with in some cases bent top and bottom chords, which were all to be welded together. In the curved sections of the roof in the transitional area to the Double Cone, the nodes of the top and bottom chords did not lie one over the other, resulting in warped trusses with bent chords and diagonals tending randomly in all directions.

The basic idea behind the special proposal was to optimize the system in terms of economical realization and practical implementation at the construction site. Despite the irregular roof structure, standard support elements were to be utilized to the greatest extent possible while still respecting and realizing the original idea behind the design. In consultation with the contractor, the irregular, in some cases warped truss structures were first transformed into vertical truss panels with joints arranged vertically on top of one another and in some areas straight truss braces running from joint to joint. This made is possible to achieve a support structure that is comparable to the straight support elements in a girder grid and which during practical realization can be broken down into single orthogonal truss panels.

Double trusses at intervals of five meters were chosen as the main support lines. These are for the most part arranged orthogonally at a distance of ten or 15 meters from each other. Between them are simple auxiliary supports in the form of underhung binders, which transfer the roof loads to the main support elements. All truss panels were produced mainly with conventional open rolled

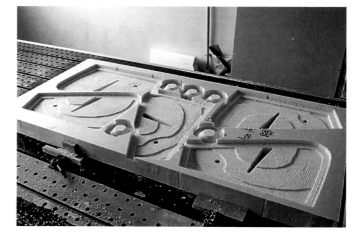

The digitized working models in turn form the basis for new physical models created with a 3D milling machine.

sections. Only for the very slim pressure diagonals with their correspondingly greater risk of buckling were pipes with various cross sections employed.

After the roof, whose support structure was originally conceived as a visible construction, had been further developed in its function alongside the lighting and physical construction conditions, it was possible to realize the economic optimization potential. As already mentioned above, the underside of the Hall roof can, depending on the lighting situation, give the impression of being either a physical body or partially transparent. High demands were no longer placed on the details of the support structure. Therefore, considerations as to fabrication, transport and assembly techniques could now take priority in designing the joints. Due to what is in some cases the extreme height of the truss structures, few elements could be delivered to the construction site as prefabricated, welded units. The majority of the structure had to be delivered to the site in the form of individual parts and put together on site in assembly guides. To speed up assembly and systematize the workflows, all assembly links were designed as bolted connections with high-strength bolts.

Despite the irregular roof structure in which no truss rod is like any other, the connections between the rods were largely standardized. A type catalogue was developed for this purpose, which considerably facilitated determining the joint connections when creating the construction drawings. Since the special proposal was worked out in detail at a time when the building shell was already being erected, special attention had to be paid to planning the steel construction in a way that was compatible with the solid building elements.

It was especially difficult to plan the connection points between the steel construction and the solid building cores and supports due to the roof structure with its vast free-spanned expanses.

It thus turned out, for example, that the columns could not be borne as originally planned on front plates with bolted connections, as usually deployed in structural engineering. Instead, the skewing of the bearing points, which was in some cases increased even further by eccentric supports that diverged from the grid, called for resting these nodes on tilting bases that allowed for the restraint-free movements of the roof structure. The connections to the solid building cores had to be realized in such a way that, on the one hand, the load-bearing conditions planned in the structural engineering could be implemented free of restraints and, on the other hand, the limiting conditions of the solid building with its unavoidable structural tolerances enabled trouble-free execution on site.

In the course of planning, and after several rounds of consultation with the inspecting engineer, it was found that, due to the substantial relative shifts in the individual systems, the original separation of the structural engineering systems for the regular roof with the Double Cone from the Lounge could not or not adequately reflect the essential limiting conditions and interplay between the systems. For this reason, extensive additional calculations were necessary to take account of this interaction.

On the whole, it was demonstrated that, due to the softness of the systems, particularly in the horizontal direction, particular attention had to be paid to the distortions and warping of the structure and that for this reason the limiting conditions of the 3D model had to be painstakingly implemented in the design of the bearing and coupling points as well.

Working models: Study models for view from below

Construction of the roof

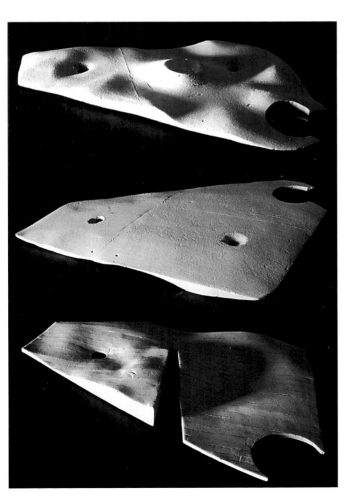

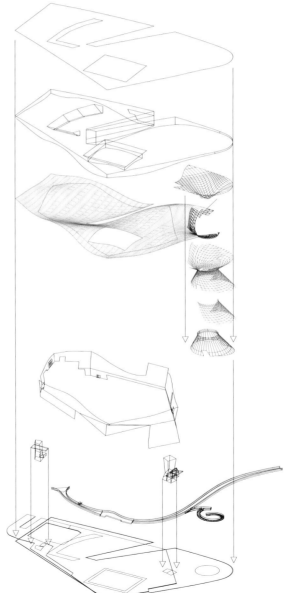

View from above
Type 21/23/25/27

Narrow ends
Type 28/29

View of Double Cone from below
Type 34

View from below, inside/outside
Type 34/35

Cone facade, Double Cone
Type 04

Sun shield
Type 04.1

Dazzle shield, Double Cone
Type 08.1

Facade
Type 01

Entrance structures N/S
Type 10

Bridge, inside/outside

Development of the roof form with the help of models and taking account of the technical and structural framework conditions

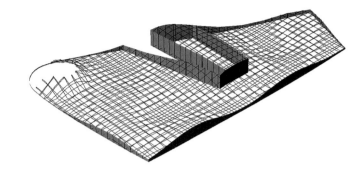

In the special proposal for the Double Cone, the main change was a halving of the interval between the originally planned ascending profiles, and the use of rectangular pipes instead of round ones, with directly applied glass panes. A secondary structure for the glazing was thus no longer necessary.

Special demands were placed on assembling the regular roof. From the viewpoint of assembly, the regular roof is separated by the break in the middle of the glass roof and the Lounge into two large, almost independent surfaces, one in the area of the Double Cone toward the Tower and the other north of the Lounge over the Forum. The girders themselves are trusses of various heights, from around 2.5 meters to over 15 meters depending on the thickness of the cloud. The southern girder grid encircles the Tower like a large plate with a hole in it and reaches to the Double Cone. It is borne only by a few isolated columns and spans the large area in front of the Tower of around 80 meters without supports. It is only capable of bearing loads after being completely assembled.

Assembly was thus carried out using assembly towers arranged to take advantage of the largest possible spans for the individual grid girders. The assembly towers supported the bottom chords of the truss braces and stabilized the up to 15-meter-high truss panels of the girders using laterally extended guides. Between 15 and 20 meters in height, the assembly towers not only took over the assembly loads but also had a reinforcement function and transferred the wind load during construction. The assembly towers were truss towers with a footprint of 3.5 x 5.0 meters. The head of the assembly tower was adapted to the respective geometry of the binders, while the base points were anchored in the steel-reinforced concrete floor over U0 (corresponding to zero level). Following completion of the

girder grid, including the connections to the load-bearing roof panel and the links to the Double Cone, the Restaurant core and the P5/P6 elevator shaft, along with the few columns, the assembly towers were relieved of their load and the support system using the girder grid activated.

The process of transferring the load was done according to a precisely calculated pattern so that the assembly towers that remained were not overloaded. In the process, four presses had to be steered synchronously for each assembly tower. In the transitional area to the Double Cone, the system changeover was accomplished in coordination with the breakdown of the guide scaffolding for the Double Cone. After the load had been switched over, the girder grid carried the load by itself and took over the static panel function between the reinforcing cores. The regular roof section north of the Lounge over the Forum was assembled the same way. In its final state, this part of the roof rests in two places on the northern truss system of the Lounge and on individual columns over the Forum.

Horizontally, the girder grid is coupled with the Lounge via knuckle-joint rods. The connection to the Lounge could not be made until the Lounge was in the final stage and the rotation movements had subsided. In this phase, the roof including the complete covering therefore had to rest on the assembly towers until, after the Lounge assembly, the horizontal and vertical coupling and load transfer process from the assembly towers could be undertaken. Only after the roof areas were connected and took up their own loads and were then united with all cores, the Double Cone and the Lounge, was the entire system stable enough to take on its final state. Through the roof panel formed at the top chord level of the girder grids, the horizontal loads are distributed among the few reinforcing cores.

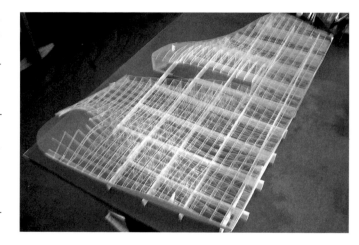

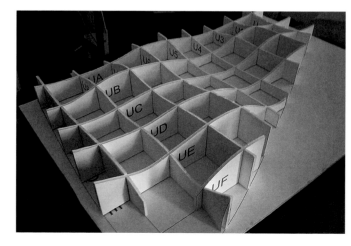

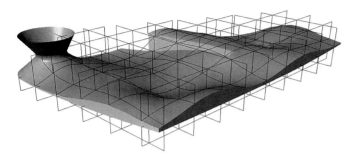

Special challenges likewise had to be mastered in the realization of technical equipment. The roof had to be completely accessible for maintenance as well as for dramatization work. The structural clearances necessary for this purpose, together with the required routes, had to be pursued continuously in three dimensions in the planning process.

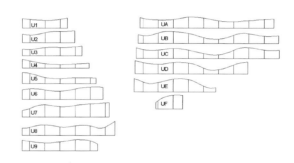

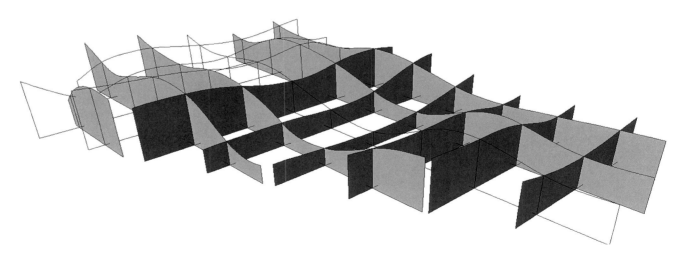

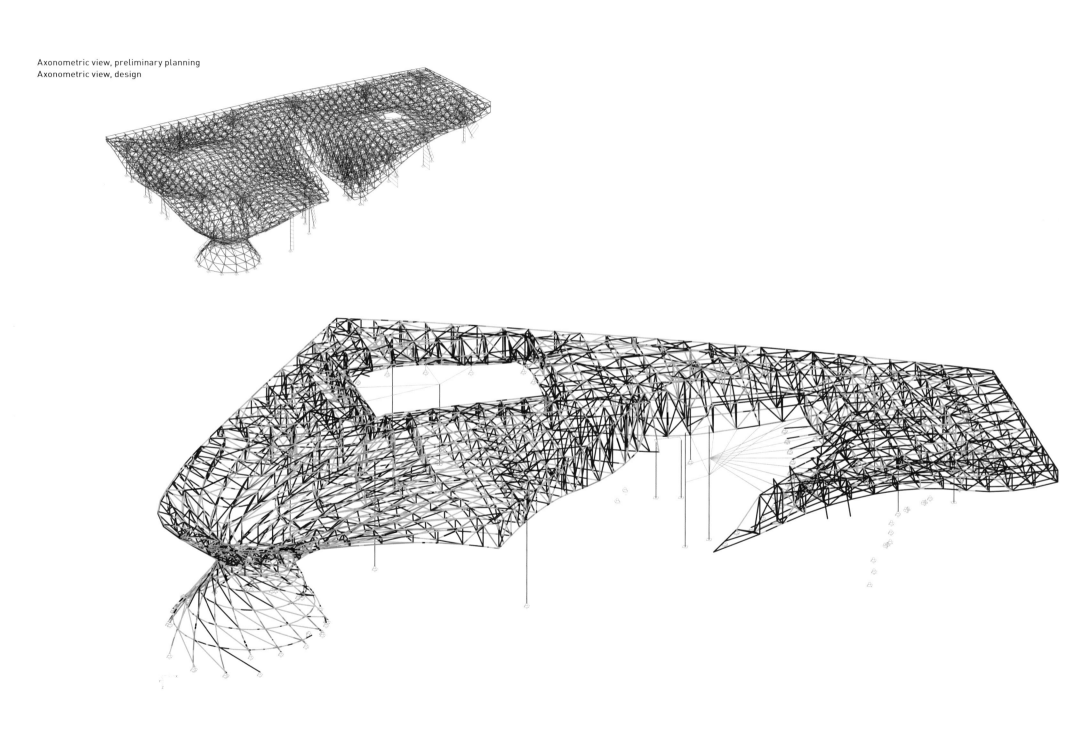

Axonometric view, preliminary planning
Axonometric view, design

Axonometric view of the structure as executed

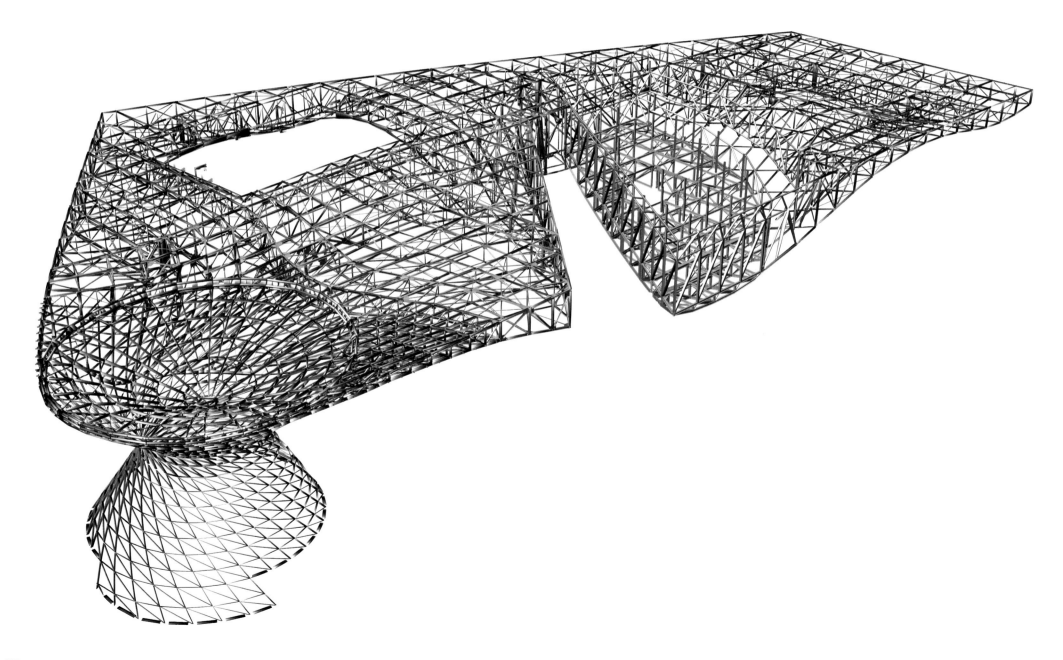

Axonometric view of the steel structure depicting the installations and service walkways, etc. The roof structure is made up of latticework in 3D. All elements built into this structure, such as maintenance catwalks, ventilation and electrical conduits, sprinklers, etc. had to be planned in 3D using CAD and examined for possible collisions.

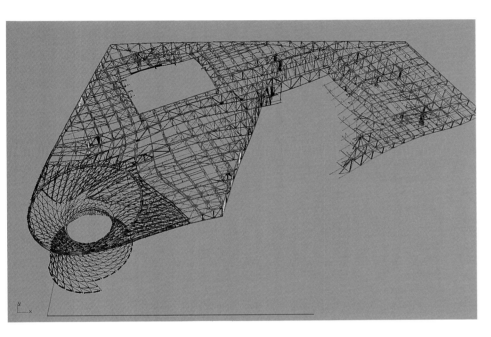

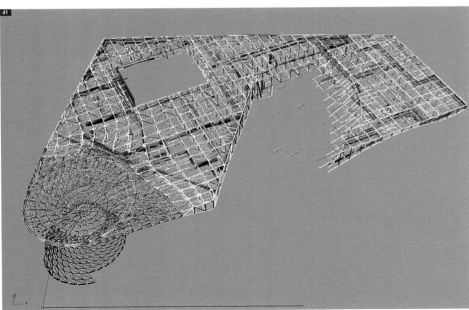

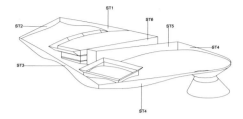

SÜDWEST / SÜDOST (DÄMMEBENE) = ST4

SÜDWEST / SÜDOST (LOCHBLECHEBENE) = ST4

INNENHAUT: DÄMMKASSETTEN/ LAMELLEN

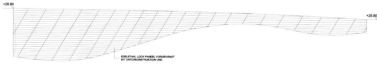

OST (DÄMMEBENE) = ST1

NORD (DÄMMEBENE) = ST2

AUSSENHAUT: LOCHBLECH

OST (LOCHBLECHEBENE) = ST1

NORD (LOCHBLECHEBENE) = ST2

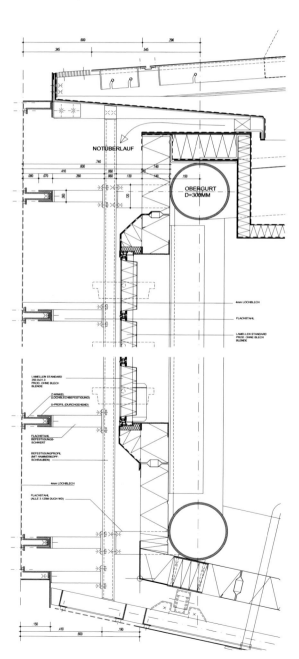

04.09.2007

04.09.2007

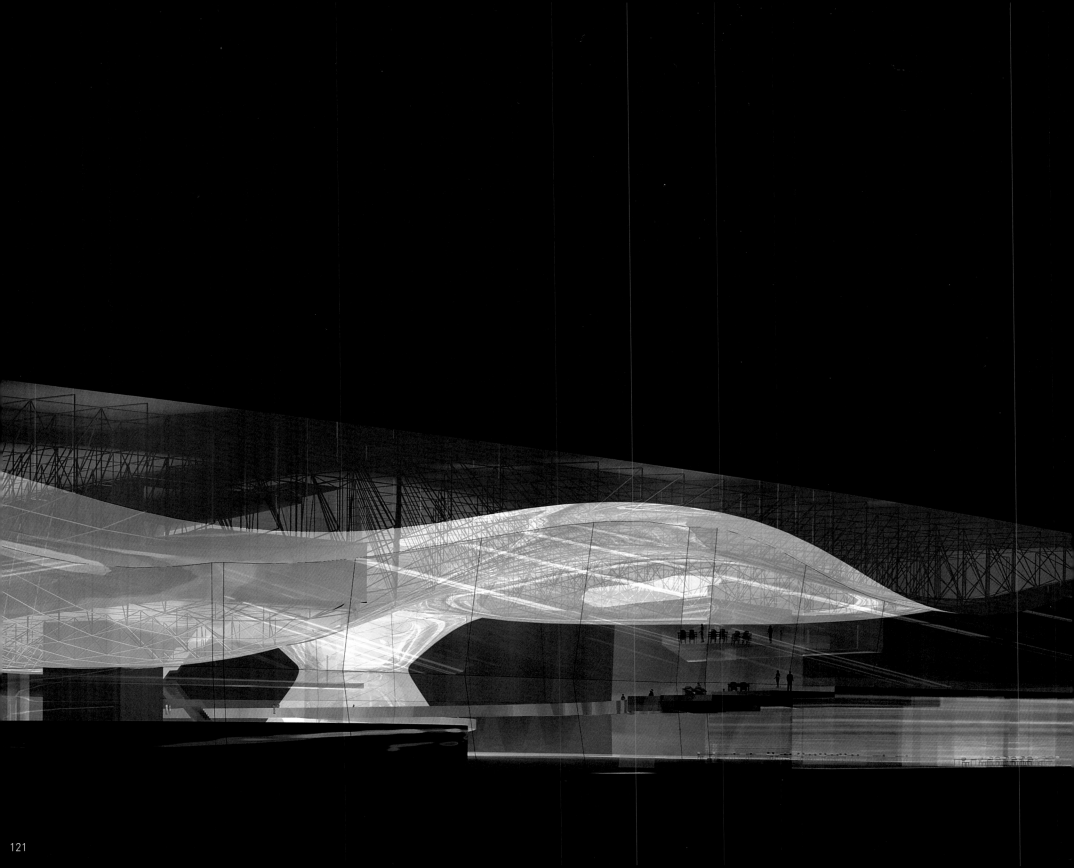

19.06.2007

Previous pages: The special twilight and nighttime effects are created by deploying variably colored lighting in the underside of the roof. The stainless steel sheeting can give either a solid or transparent impression depending on the way it is lit.

Panel division of the stainless steel, view from below

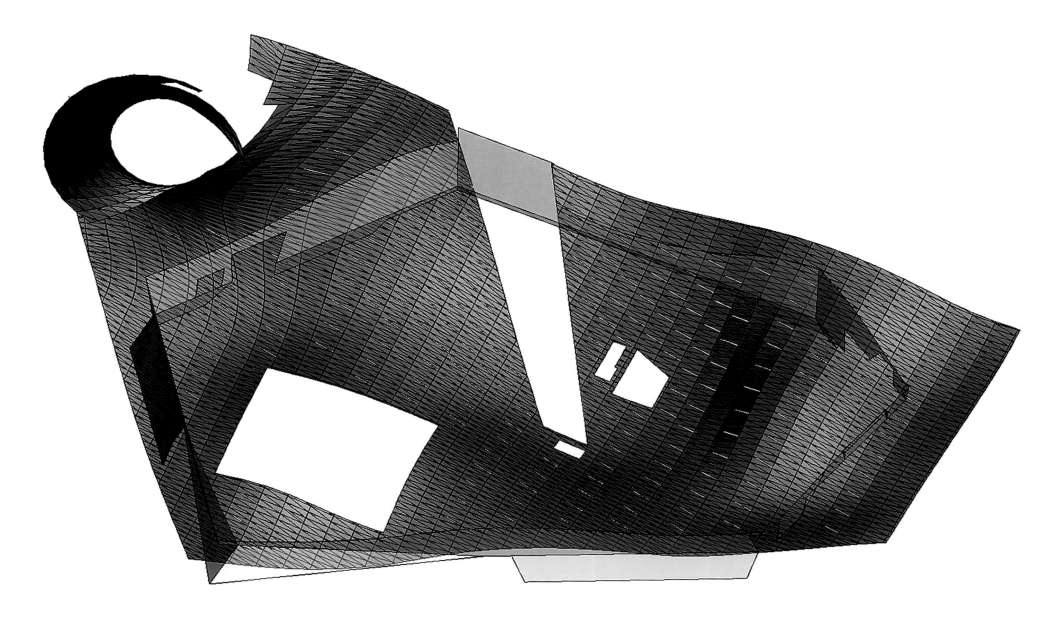

The lamps used in the light slits meet all criteria for stage lighting.
The densest cluster of lights is located in the Premiere area.

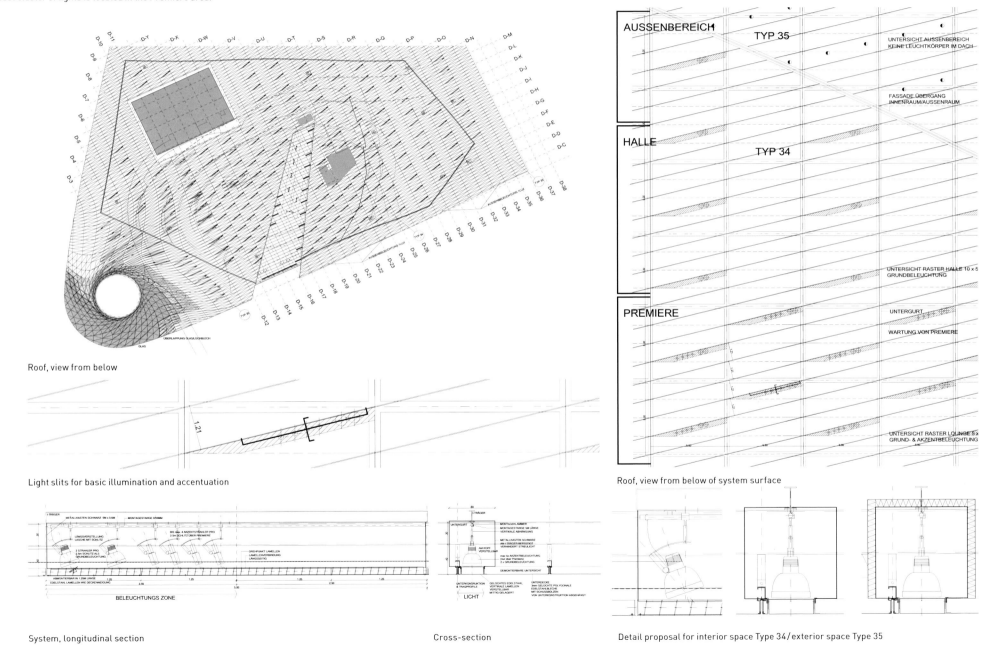

Roof, view from below

Light slits for basic illumination and accentuation

System, longitudinal section

Cross-section

Roof, view from below of system surface

Detail proposal for interior space Type 34/exterior space Type 35

22.02.2007

Due to the complex geometry of the underside of the roof, all light boxes and
the lighting elements inside them had to be planned in 3D using CAD.

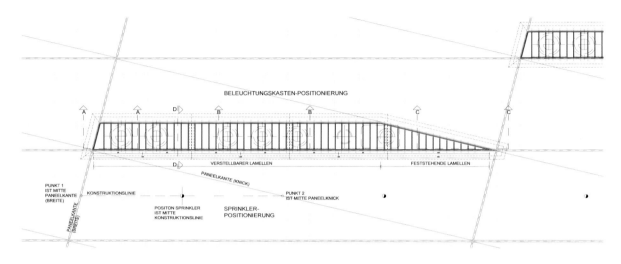

BELEUCHTUNGSKASTEN-POSITIONIERUNG

VERSTELLBARER LAMELLEN   FESTSTEHENDE LAMELLEN

PANEELKANTE (KNICK)

PUNKT 1
IST MITTE
PANEELKANTE
(BREITE)   KONSTRUKTIONSLINIE   PUNKT 2
                                          IST MITTE PANEELKNICK

POSITON SPRINKLER
IST MITTE   SPRINKLER-
KONSTRUKTIONSLINIE   POSITIONIERUNG

View of roof from below; system surface with placing of lighting and sprinklers

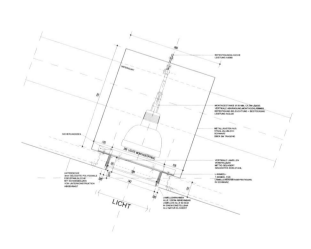

View of roof from below

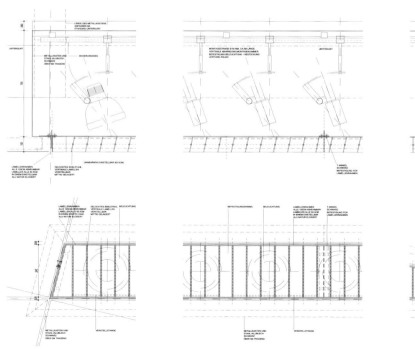

Zone A (adjustable)   Zone B (adjustable)   Zone C (fixed)

Section D–D

LICHT

Regulatory details: roof edge and view from below, exterior

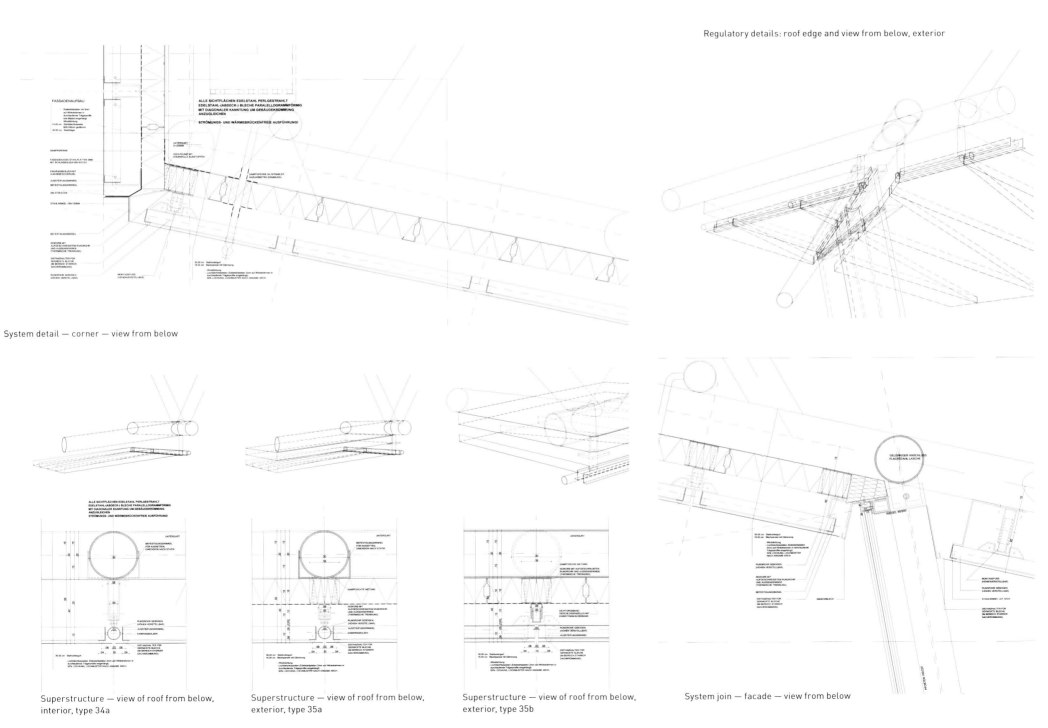

System detail — corner — view from below

Superstructure — view of roof from below, interior, type 34a

Superstructure — view of roof from below, exterior, type 35a

Superstructure — view of roof from below, exterior, type 35b

System join — facade — view from below

10.05.2006

3

The facade was conceived as a modified post-and-beam system. Leaning ten degrees out of the vertical, the posts are bent at a height of 7.50 meters. The advantage of the bent construction is that vertical warping of the roof can be taken up by the elastic bending of the posts. This eliminated the need for movement joints in the roof. The posts are coupled with the roof structure at both the top and bottom chord levels. Where the variably running roof edge is higher, the facade is in addition braced against the roof at a height of 15 meters. This reduces the free span widths to the extent that only minimal post cross-sections are required in relation to the height of the facade. The facade posts are placed at intervals of 5 meters. The facade cross-sections consist of two coupled flat steel plates in order to afford hidden routing and easy accessibility in the posts for the building services supply lines.

The horizontal beams are placed at intervals of 2.5 meters. They connect to the posts eccentrically and take the form of welded triangular profiles that take up only the stresses caused by the wind. The beams at a height of 7.45 meters and 15.0 meters are connected to each other in a tension- and pressure-resistant manner in order to keep the facade posts in the facade plane and prevent them from buckling out. Otherwise, they are connected in the regular area through longitudinal holes. In order to model the actual warping of the roof, the exterior loads and the thermal forces exerted on the jointless facade structure, the facade was studied using a modified roof/Double Cone model. The beams at a height of 7.45 meters and 15.0 meters were connected in the respective facade planes to the components that perforate the facade or to the roof. In order to minimize the horizontal warping of the facade corners, the elements supporting the roof inside were coordinated with the facade corners. This makes it possible to calculate the proportion of the roof warping that is relevant for the bent facade even for the areas that geometrically diverge from the regular facade. The overall system of the facade structure was also represented as a spatial skeleton structure. The procedure for producing proof of structural engineering soundness was similar to that for the roof support structure. The glazing is clamped directly to the beams and glued in the butt joints. It was slogged as closely to the edge as possible in order to minimize bending loads from the beams.

The facade, with its average height of around 22 meters and the geometric demands posed by a "bending point" and the limiting conditions of the structure that had to be observed (such as the warping behavior of the roof construction or the influence of the facade heating), presented a level of difficulty that can hardly be appreciated at first glance. In variance from the initial design approach, a vertically shiftable connection to the roof was selected to ensure that any vertical warping in the roof structure would not lead to hard-to-control forces and deformations in the posts. The axial grid is 5.0 meters wide and around 2.5 meters high. The large-format (2.5 x 5.0 meter) glass elements set into it have a line- and point-supported anchoring and were selected according to the maximum producible size. In order to examine the various facade systems (different system heights, some sections with and some without intermediate supports, diverse expansion joints, some permeable effects, etc.) a number of partial models were created. The expected internal force variables and distortions were determined on the basis of these models.

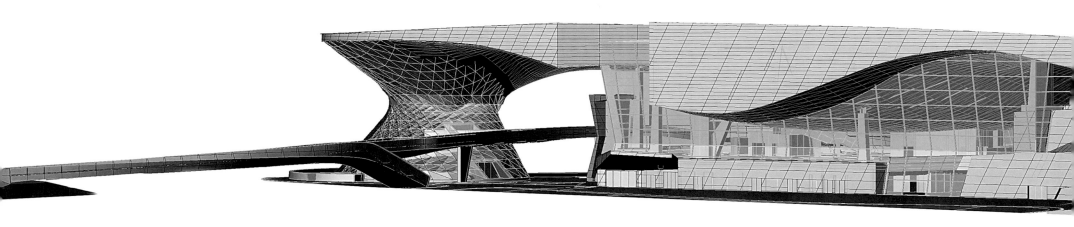

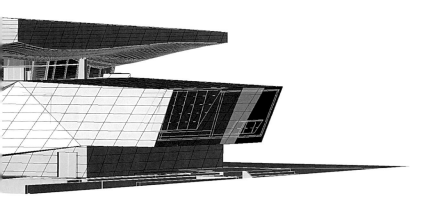

North-east aspect
North aspect

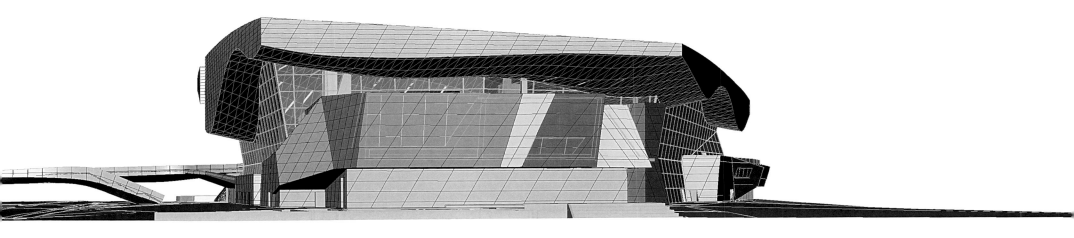

South-west aspect
North-west aspect

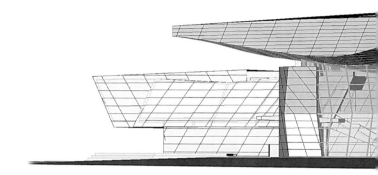

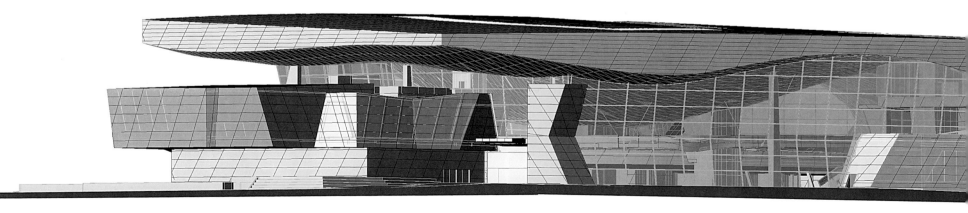

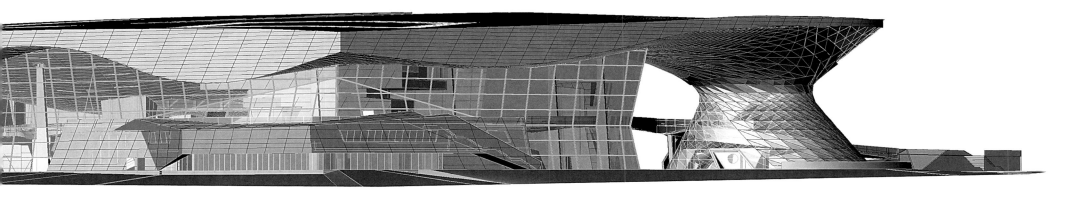

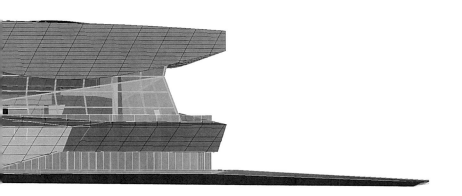

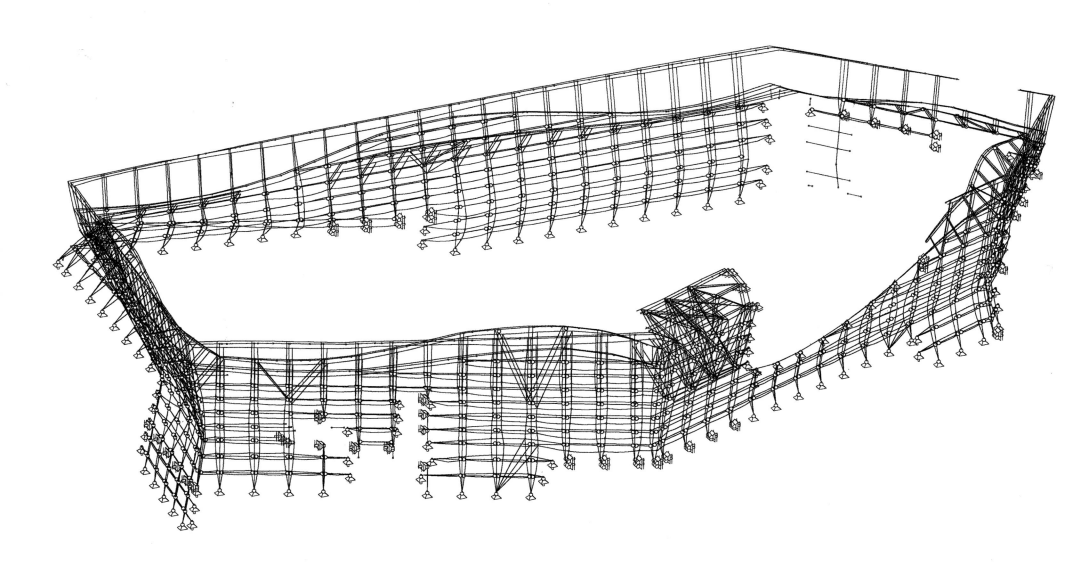

Axonometric view of the entire facade showing the support conditions

10.05.2005

In the vertical hollow profiles of the facade hot water circulates in order
to prevent the descent of cold air in winter.

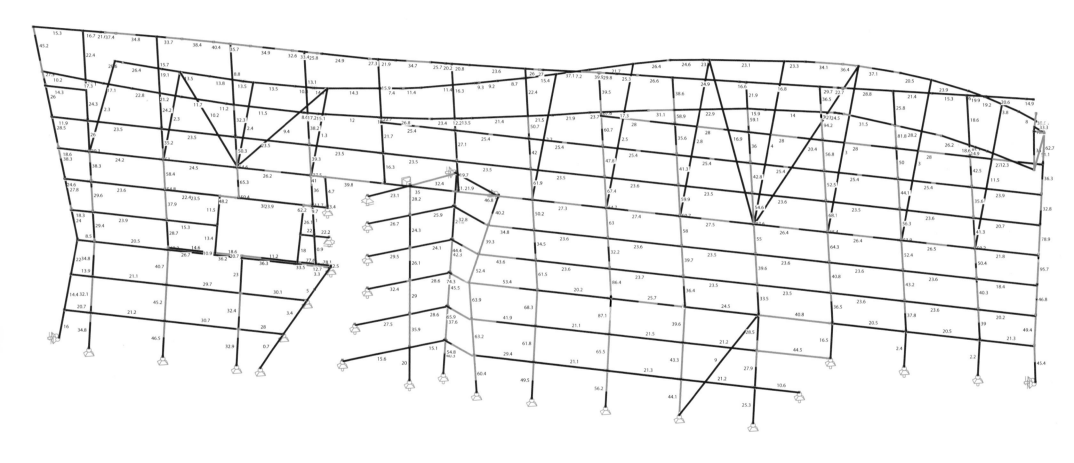

Through the bend and the additional protrusion from the roof structure,
the free span of the facade trusses were reduced to a third of the
original length, enabling an especially lean design.

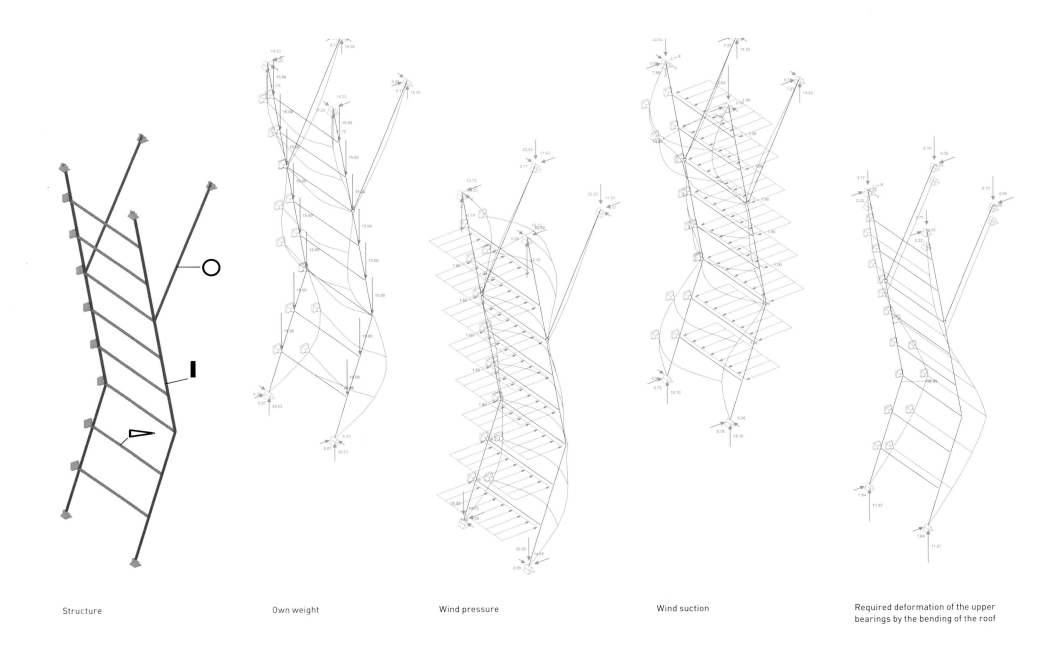

Structure

Own weight

Wind pressure

Wind suction

Required deformation of the upper
bearings by the bending of the roof

16.03.2006

143

Facade sections in the area of the Restaurant with horizontal slats for
natural ventilation of the Hall as well as for smoke exhaust in case of fire

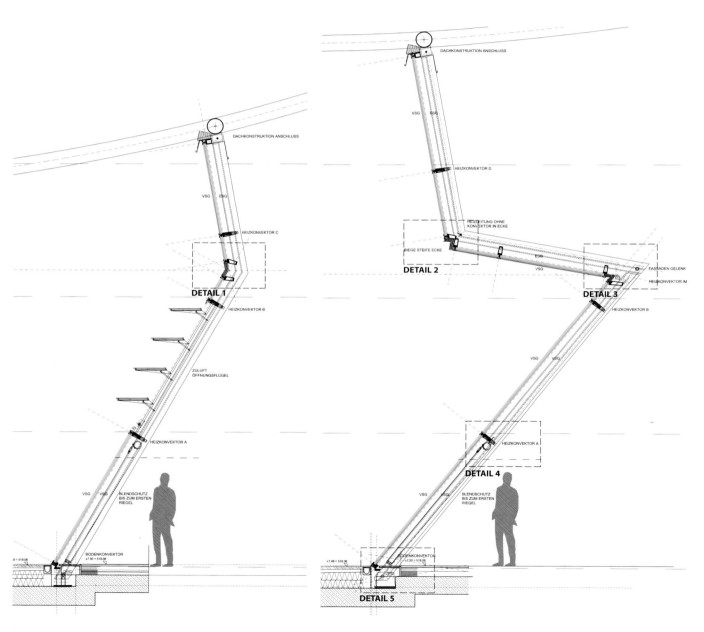

Section through west facade

Section through south-east facade; F.56

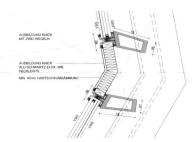

DETAIL 1

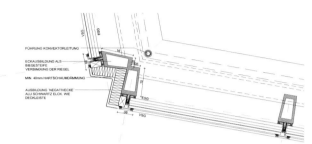

DETAIL 2

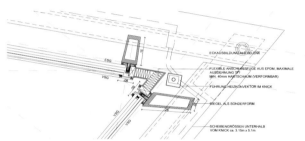

DETAIL 3

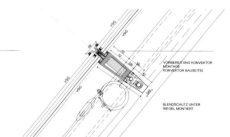

DETAIL 4

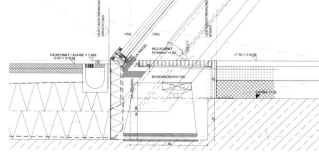

DETAIL 5

06.10.2006

Facade cross-section
Below: Hollow profiles under construction

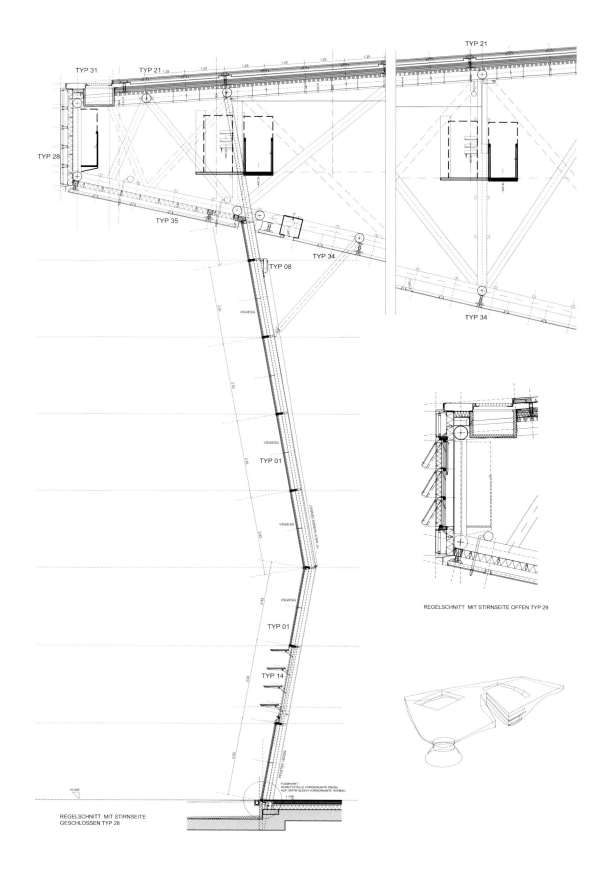

TYP 31
TYP 21
TYP 21
TYP 28
TYP 35
TYP 34
TYP 34
TYP 08
VSG/ESG
VSG/ESG
TYP 01
VSG/ESG
TYP 01
VSG/ESG
TYP 14

REGELSCHNITT MIT STIRNSEITE OFFEN TYP 29

+0.000

REGELSCHNITT MIT STIRNSEITE
GESCHLOSSEN TYP 28

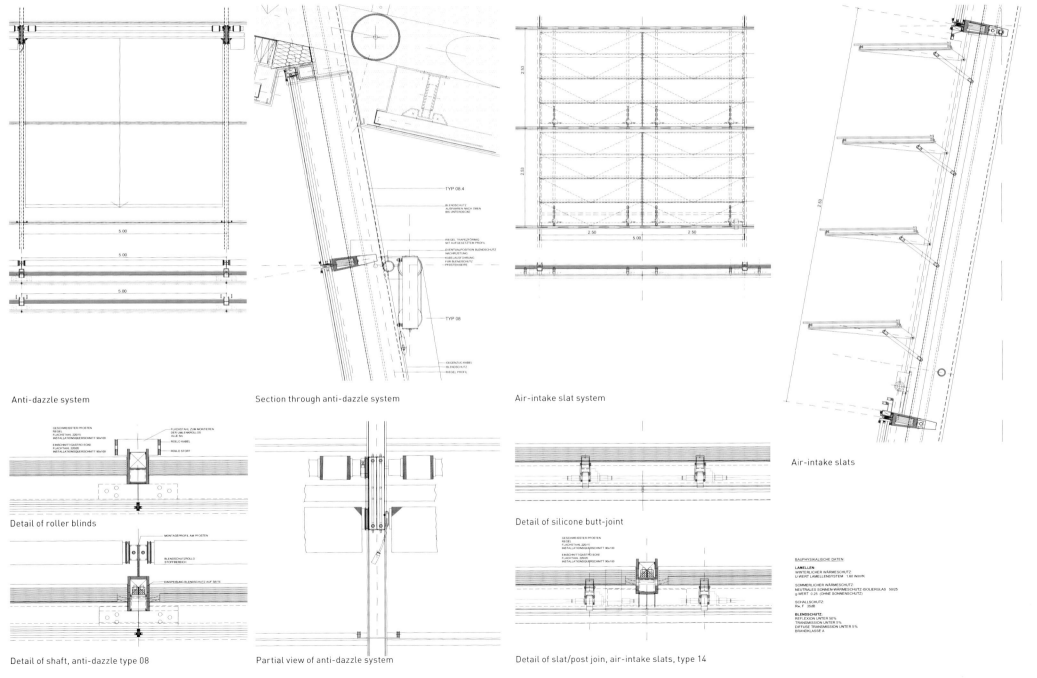

Anti-dazzle system

Section through anti-dazzle system

Air-intake slat system

Air-intake slats

Detail of roller blinds

Detail of silicone butt-joint

Detail of shaft, anti-dazzle type 08

Partial view of anti-dazzle system

Detail of slat/post join, air-intake slats, type 14

147

04.09.2007

03.09.2007

09.09.2007

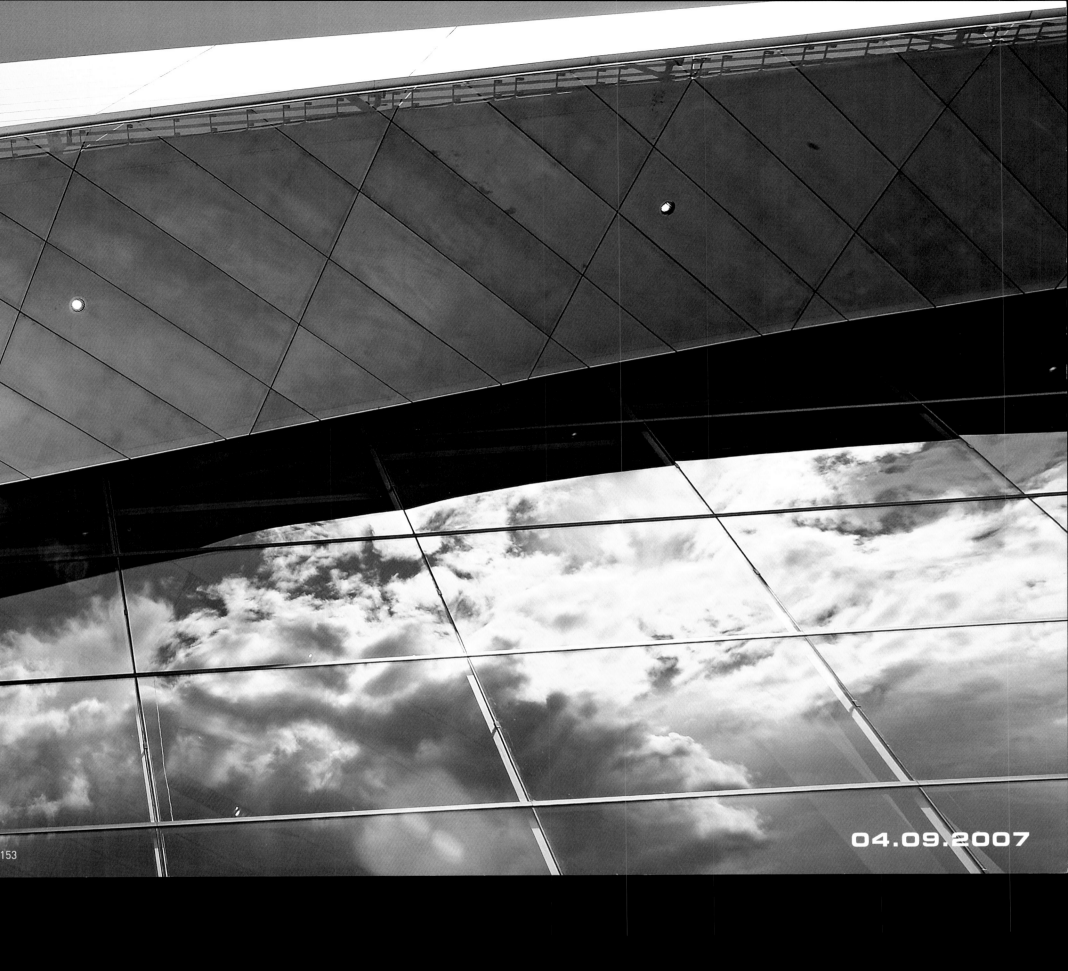

04.09.2007

4

Lounge

The Lounge section of the building is found directly above the Premiere platforms, the heart of BMW Welt, at the height of the top levels E2 to E4, so that it is positively encased in the roof cloud. Due to the larger roof volume at Level E4, this level has a larger floor plan and juts about 6 meters over the floor below. The entire structure, which measures 70 x 34 meters on Level E3 and 70 x 40 meters on Level E4, was planned to rest on only five points so as not to interfere with the Premiere area on Level E1. Based on these limiting conditions, a "load-bearing box" was developed with load-bearing panels and walls in the form of the floor slabs and the surrounding story-high lattice girders. Four of the five load transfer points are found on the longitudinal sides in the vicinity of the surrounding lattice girders. The fifth load transfer point is the internal core with its torsion-resistant cross-section, which at the same time also ensures the necessary bracing.

The roof of the Lounge and the ceiling over Level E3 are executed using composite beams, adjusted to a grid size of 5 x 10 meters. These rest on the composite columns, the surrounding lattice girders and directly on the core. The loads borne by the composite columns are taken up by the lattice grid of the fish-bellied girder, the top chord level of which is likewise bonded to the steel-reinforced concrete ceiling panel above. The encircling, in some parts glazed lattice and the internal core rest in the north on two large steel-reinforced columns and in the south on inclined console-like steel composite structures in the elevator panels. Through these "oblique" intersections at the load transfer points and the great load forces exerted (up to 12,000 KN), high horizontal forces arose that had to be borne through the concrete ceiling panel via the fish-bellied girder level and on into the core.

Furthermore, the horizontal and vertical loads had to be conducted from the adjacent roof to the cantilevered lattice girders on the north side of the Lounge. Through this load and the eccentric load discharge, additional large horizontal stresses were conducted into the floor slab panels. These horizontal loads are conducted by the steel construction into the concrete floor slabs and from these on into the core. With this complex stress on the floor slabs, as well as on the composite beams, it is necessary to design the above-mentioned components to withstand this unusual sequence of forces (large panel strain, bending with normal force for the composite beams).

Due to the geometry, the stresses and the construction of the Lounge, it was necessary to support the Lounge on assembly towers and then to subject it to its load only when complete. In order to carry out the ceiling lowering process in this highly complex support system with as few restraints as possible and to ensure optimal assembly, the bearing points for the composite beams were executed on the core as freely rotating bearing pockets. Moreover, a ceiling strip between the core and the southern lattice girder, which runs through the middle of the field approx. three meters from the core, was covered in concrete only after the lowering procedure.

The support structure of the Lounge was likewise modeled as a three-dimensional framework (figure 15). The structural engineering evidence was provided in accordance with the procedure described above. The Lounge was not part of the special design proposals and was realized according to the original plans. Two full floors of over 2,000 square meters each rest atop the so-called "fish-bellied girder level," a girder grid construction that conveys the floor loads into the encircling, structure-high main lattice girders. The bearing points consist on the south side of a "finger construction" projecting obliquely from the lateral elevator shaft, which through its inclination generates up to 7 MN in horizontal forces from 14 MN in vertical loads.

On the north side are two slanted steel-reinforced concrete columns. Only the torsion-resistant central core with stairwell and elevators is able to give the system global stability. On the north side, the encircling main lattice grid is bent and pivoted between the two floors, yielding two nearly independent, variously bent lattice grids that are only one story high. On the south, east and west sides, the supporting main lattice girders reach from the fish-bellied girder level over both floors up to the roof. The static load-bearing capacity of the Lounge was reached only after complete assembly in conjunction with the cores, the Premiere platform (a large steel-reinforced concrete slab below the Lounge) and the load-bearing Lounge decks.

21.10.2005

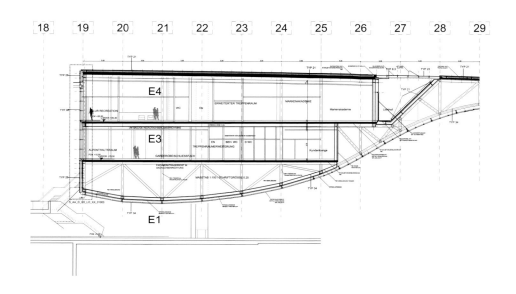

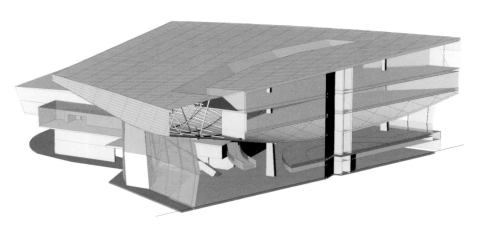

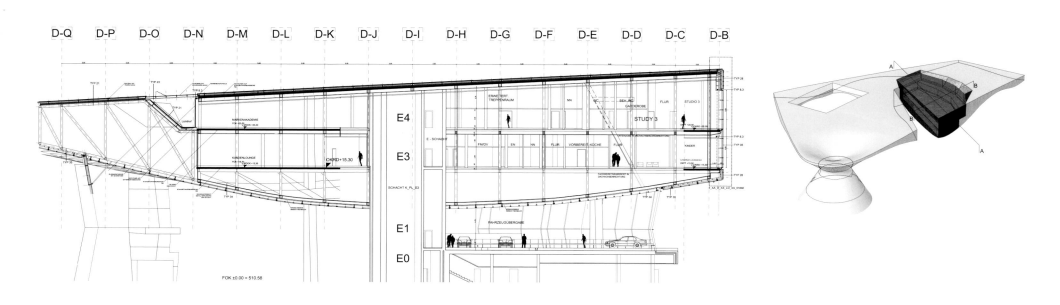

24.08.2006

Detail sections, Lounge

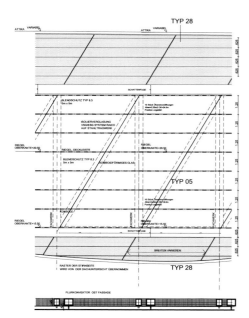

Lounge facade: standard surface

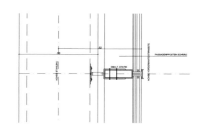

Buffering, primary: bolt

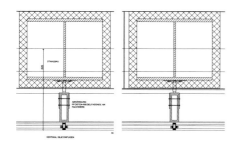

Buffering, primary: silicone join

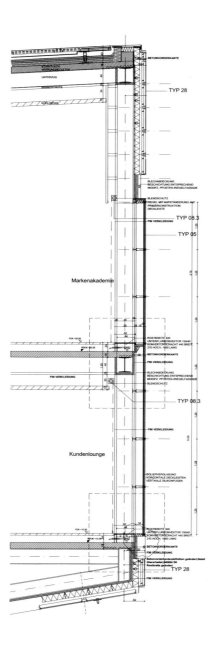

Standard section, vertical

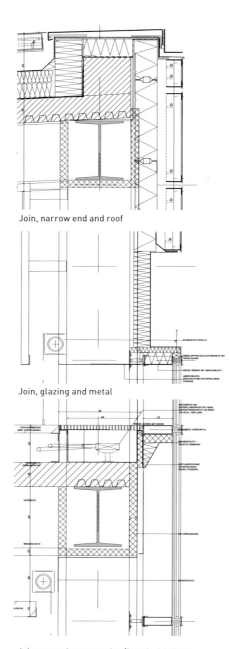

Join, narrow end and roof

Join, glazing and metal

Join, ground construction/facade 4th floor
Standard section, details

09.08.2006

161

Longitudinal section: staircase, Lounge
Below: Ground plan: staircase, Lounge

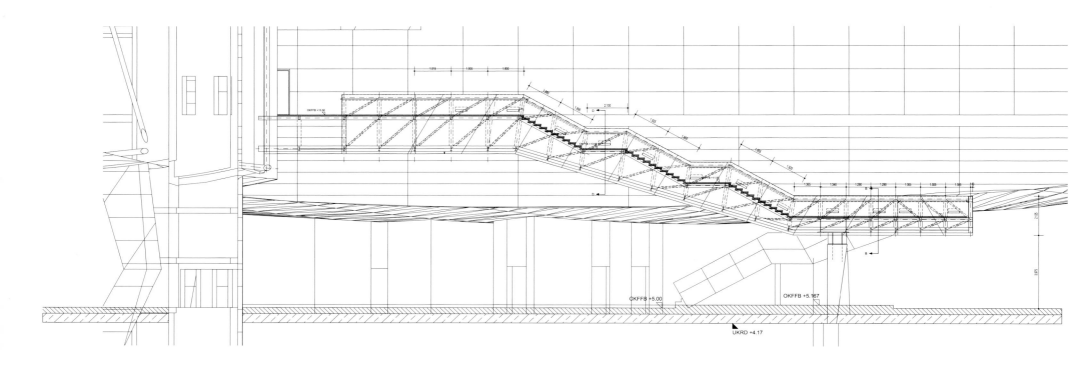

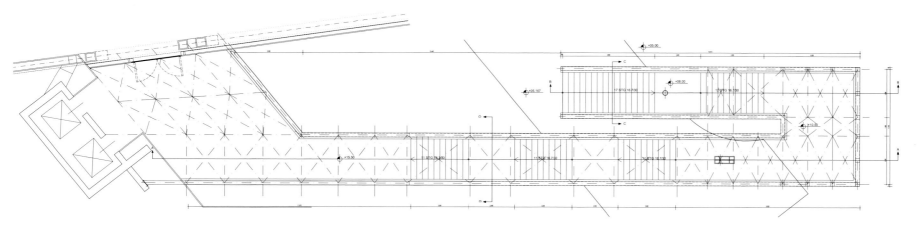

03.09.2007

04.09.2007

5

Dynamism and elegance play a major role in today's architectural discourse. The design paradigms for BMW Welt thus called for the portrayal of the dynamic forces of a situation of overstress in an elegant fashion. The design idea behind the bridge, which allows the street to be crossed on foot and connects BMW Welt to the Museum, as well as linking the functional areas within BMW Welt, was to expand the space in BMW Welt.

Therefore, the structure and form of the bridge outside of BMW Welt (exterior bridge) followed the form of the bridge inside (interior bridge). The functional and formal concepts were in this way extended over Lerchenauerstrasse, and the BMW areas on the opposite side (company headquarters and museum) were connected to vehicle traffic without an intersection.

Inside BMW Welt, all publicly accessible areas, such as the Forum, the Tower and the Double Cone, are connected by this bridge. In order to avoid columns in the interior, the bridge was suspended from the roof. At defined panorama points, curving bays in the bridge invite guests to pause and take in the scene. The largest span of the exterior bridge is around 60 meters. The material chosen for the outer cladding is glass-bead-blasted stainless steel — the same as the outer skin of BMW Welt.

The support structure of the footbridge that connects the various building zones consists mainly of a steel trough cross-section, the sides of which are executed as truss girders in the longitudinal bridge direction. The regular interval between the elements in the trough half-frame is three meters.

In the truss girders at the trough sides, an additional truss post is arranged between two half-frames. The bridge does not display a consistent cross-section over its entire length, since the inner railing supports are "folded out" horizontally at several junctures and replaced by a glass parapet. In addition, the underside of the bridge "dives" under the regular trough cross-section in several places. The design of these free-form areas in the support structure was used either to heighten the statically effective cross-section or as a lightweight secondary structure. The load-transfer situation of the bridge is a distinctive feature of the support structure design: with the exception of two columns in the outdoor areas, it inserts itself apparently seamlessly into the structure, since it is suspended from the roof and Lounge structure and rests on cantilevered solid construction of the Tower and Forum.

Outdoors in front of the Double Cone is the longest bridge section between two steel-reinforced concrete columns, measuring 35 meters and additionally supported by a ramp structure leading into the Double Cone. Here, the bridge leads onto a spiral staircase in the Double Cone using flexibly connected steel consoles and is borne according to the principle of the unilaterally loaded ring girder.

The walking surface of the bridge consists of orthotropic plates with a bracing metal cover panel that as a thrust field provides horizontal reinforcement and was modeled in the calculation as eccentric tension bracing. The tension braces in the trough sides are formed by flat steel profiles, or in high-stress areas by a closed metal plate whose effect was planned analogous to that of the cover plate in the calculation model.

The calculation model was likewise carried out for the entire bridge system as a spatial framework. Taking the equivalent imperfection calculation according to second-order theory, the bend lengths for the varying stiffnesses of the trough half-frame were determined for the top chord of the bridge cross-section. For the bridge support structure as well, all changes and adjustments were updated continuously in the overall model with the roof and Double Cone. This made it possible, among other things, to examine temperature restraints between the spiral staircase and the Double Cone.

07.12.2006

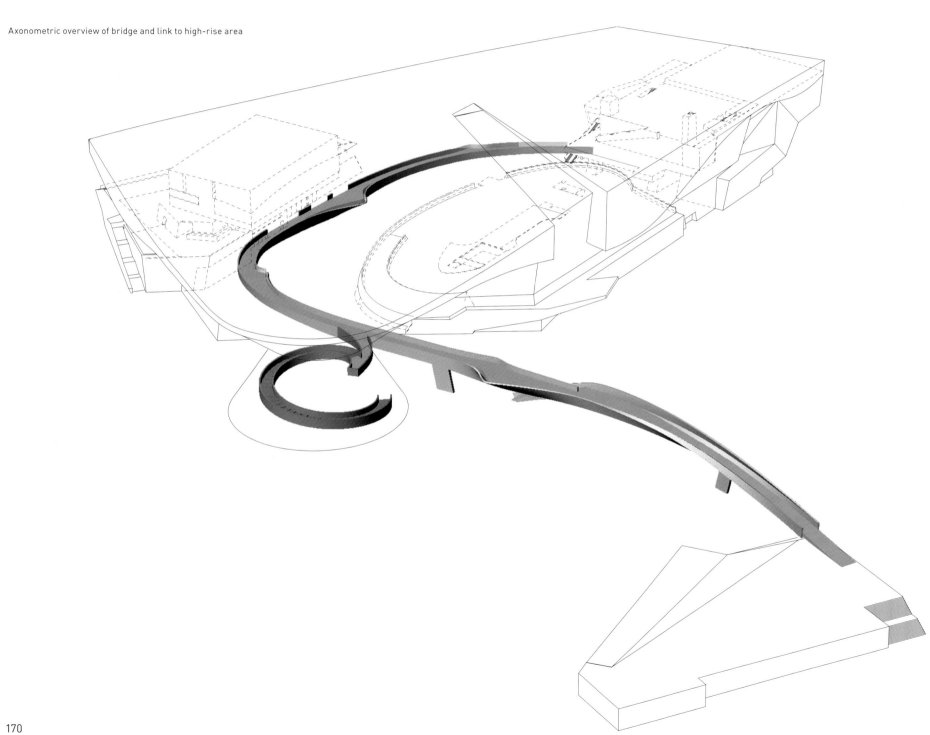

Axonometric overview of bridge and link to high-rise area

View from below: reflected ceiling plan of the interior bridge with illumination boxes

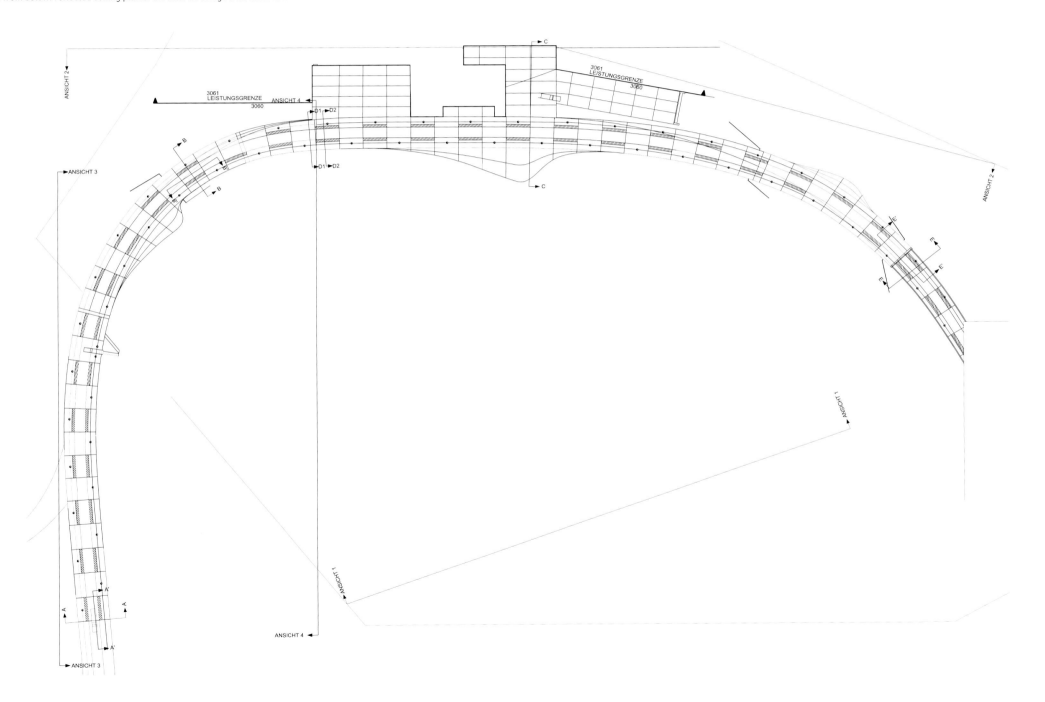

Cross-section C-C: bridge support on the Tower

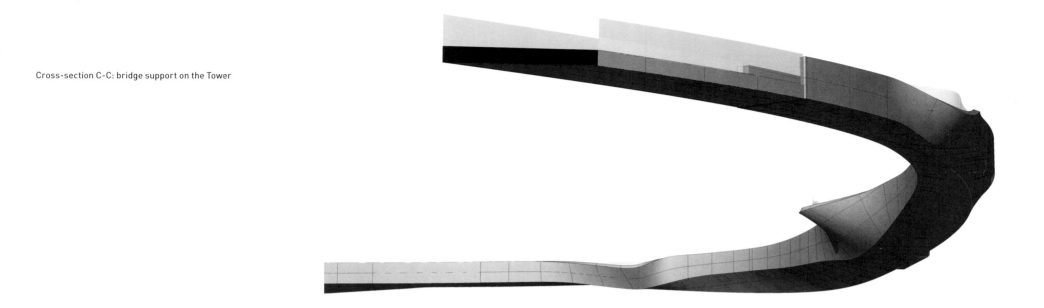

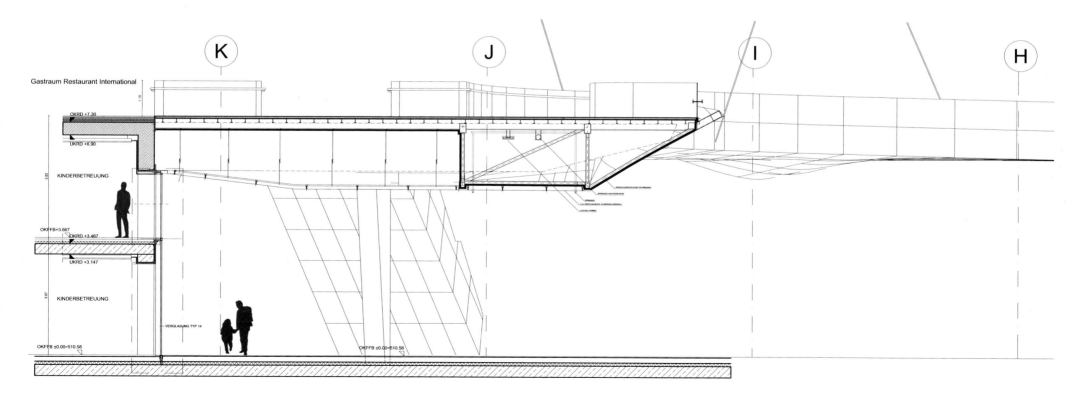

10.11.2006

View of inner and outer bridges

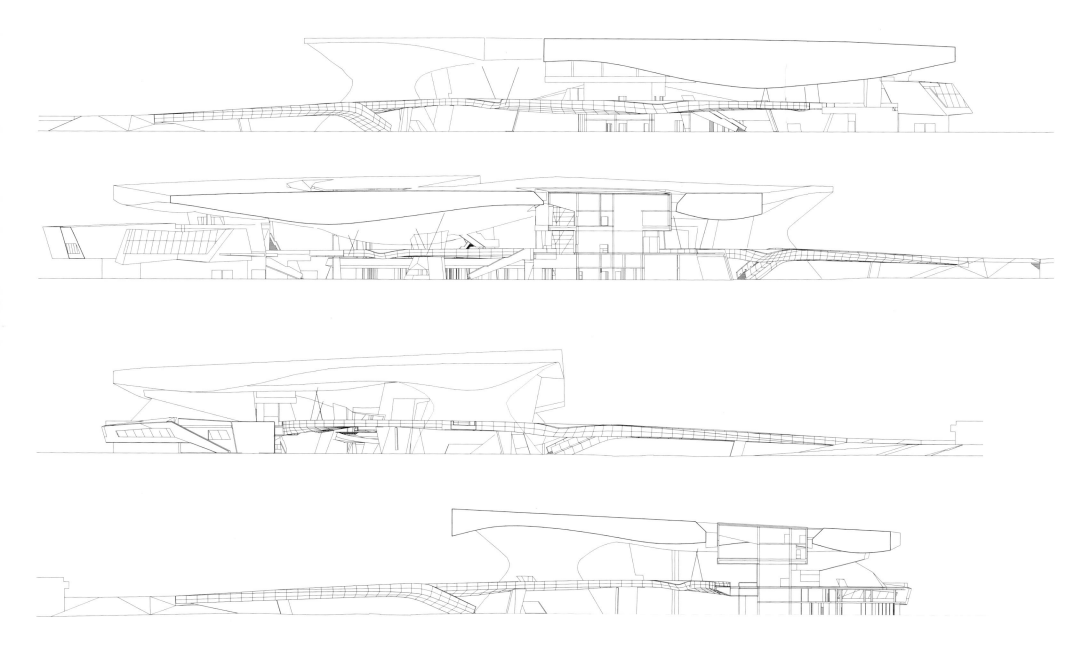

04.09.2007

20.06.2007

Standard cross-section: bridge

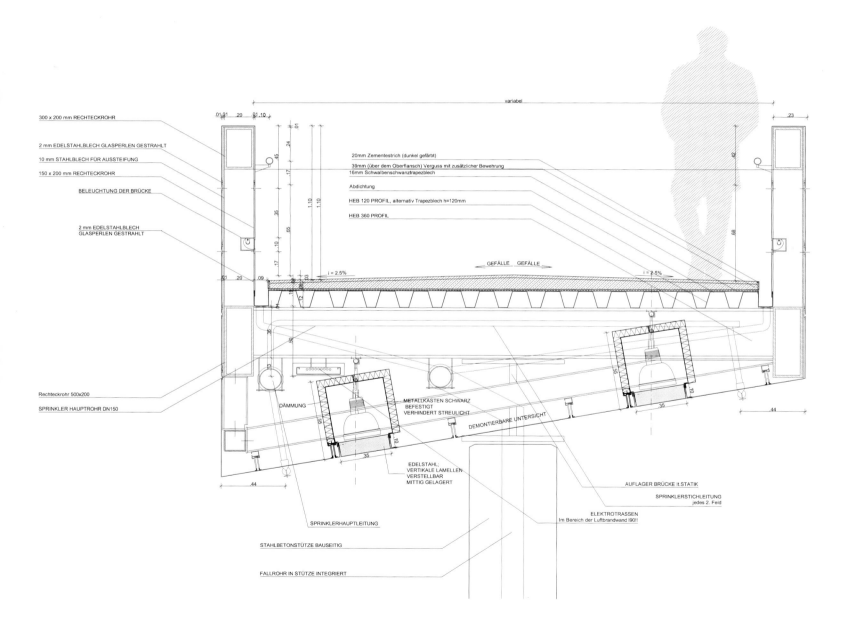

300 x 200 mm RECHTECKROHR

2 mm EDELSTAHLBLECH GLASPERLEN GESTRAHLT

10 mm STAHLBLECH FÜR AUSSTEIFUNG

150 x 200 mm RECHTECKROHR

BELEUCHTUNG DER BRÜCKE

2 mm EDELSTAHLBLECH
GLASPERLEN GESTRAHLT

Rechteckrohr 500x200

SPRINKLER HAUPTROHR DN150

variabel

20mm Zementestrich (dunkel gefärbt)

39mm (über dem Oberflansch) Verguss mit zusätzlicher Bewehrung
16mm Schwalbenschwanztrapezblech

Abdichtung

HEB 120 PROFIL, alternativ Trapezblech h=120mm

HEB 360 PROFIL

GEFÄLLE   GEFÄLLE

i = 2.5%

i = 2.5%

METALLKÄSTEN SCHWARZ
BEFESTIGT
VERHINDERT STREULICHT

DÄMMUNG

DEMONTIERBARE UNTERSICHT

EDELSTAHL;
VERTIKALE LAMELLEN
VERSTELLBAR
MITTIG GELAGERT

AUFLAGER BRÜCKE lt.STATIK

SPRINKLERSTICHLEITUNG
jedes 2. Feld

ELEKTROTRASSEN
Im Bereich der Luftbrandwand I90!!

SPRINKLERHAUPTLEITUNG

STAHLBETONSTÜTZE BAUSEITIG

FALLROHR IN STÜTZE INTEGRIERT

04.09.2007

Development of the metal cladding of the bridge

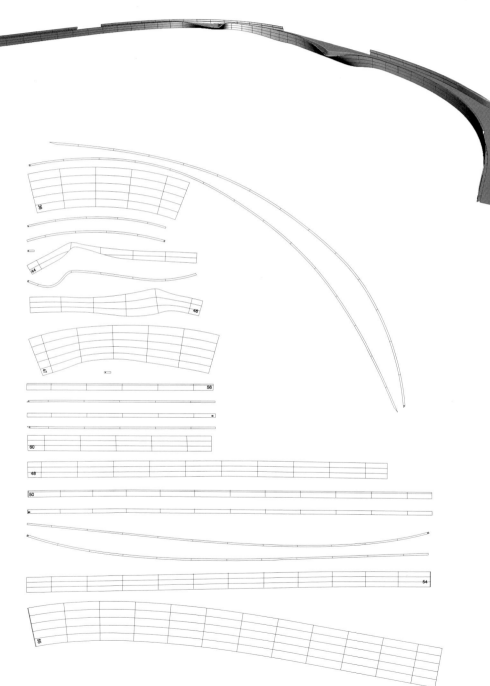

02.02.2007

04.09.2007

04.09.2007

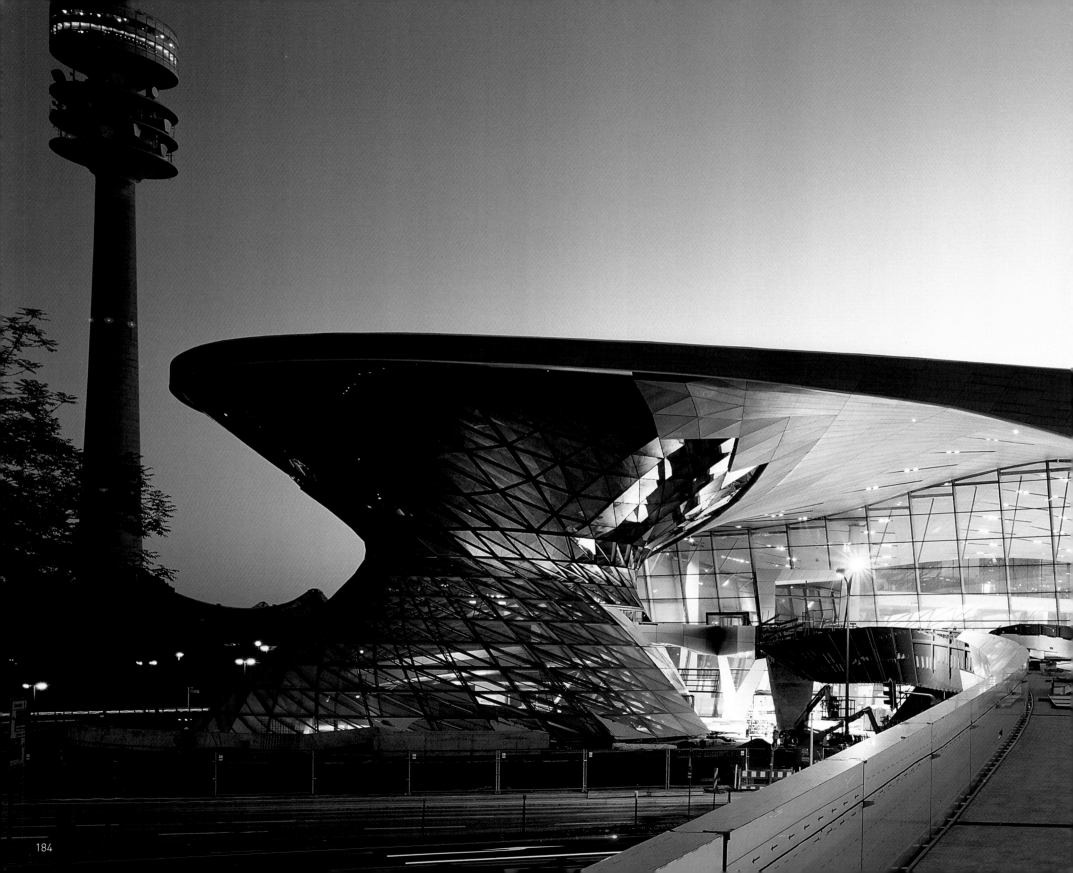

14.07.2007

6

Forum

The heart of the Forum is the large Auditorium, which is equipped with variable hydraulic platforms. The Auditorium provides a backdrop for a wide variety of possible events, from banquets to classic theater. The platform topography is made up of one-meter-wide platform strips on guide rails along the longitudinal sides of the Auditorium. These are infinitely adjustable in height using push-pull chains. The theater space thus offers maximum flexibility. Various heights can be created according to event type. The event space itself is supplemented by lateral stages, backstage and under-stage areas.

A mobile wall can be moved aside to open up the Auditorium to the Hall along its entire width. This moveable gate functions like a reversed "iron curtain," since it is not raised but rather sunk into the floor. The whole Auditorium then becomes a stage, with the boundaries between stage and audience flexibly adjustable to fit the event concerned. Since fire prevention regulations now allow audience members to be on stage, the Auditorium itself can form a vast stage without any need for fire-preventing separation measures between audience and performers. The spatial conception of the Auditorium likewise reflects these various event forms. The great quantity of technical equipment, from stage and media technology to stage lighting, had to be available in every part of the room and could thus not be hidden but was instead integrated in such a way as to have its own presence in the space. Mobile dividing walls on the side stages can be moved to turn the Auditorium into a freely playable space without specific orientation.

Another consequence of the variety of desired uses was that the Forum had to be sound-insulated from the rest of the building. Noise from the loading yard located directly below could not be al-lowed to permeate into the Forum, nor should there be any mutual disturbance between the Forum and the adjacent rooms. Vibrations from the pressing plant on the opposite side of the street also had to be eliminated as far as possible. The large Auditorium was thus realized as a "room within a room." The inner shell was floated atop Sylomer supports. The lower half of the shell is made of steel-reinforced concrete, the upper half of a multi-planked steel structure.

The Forum is supplemented by a full-service conference area that is cantilevered out 20 meters from the body of the Forum, dictating its appearance toward the north. The size of the conference rooms can be adapted for various requirements using mobile dividing walls. Because of the variety of functions and the limiting conditions of the building site, the various floor plans for the Forum levels had to be realized on jutting cantilevered areas with pre-tensioned curtain wall panels.

Depiction of the stainless-steel panel division on the Forum

09.09.2005

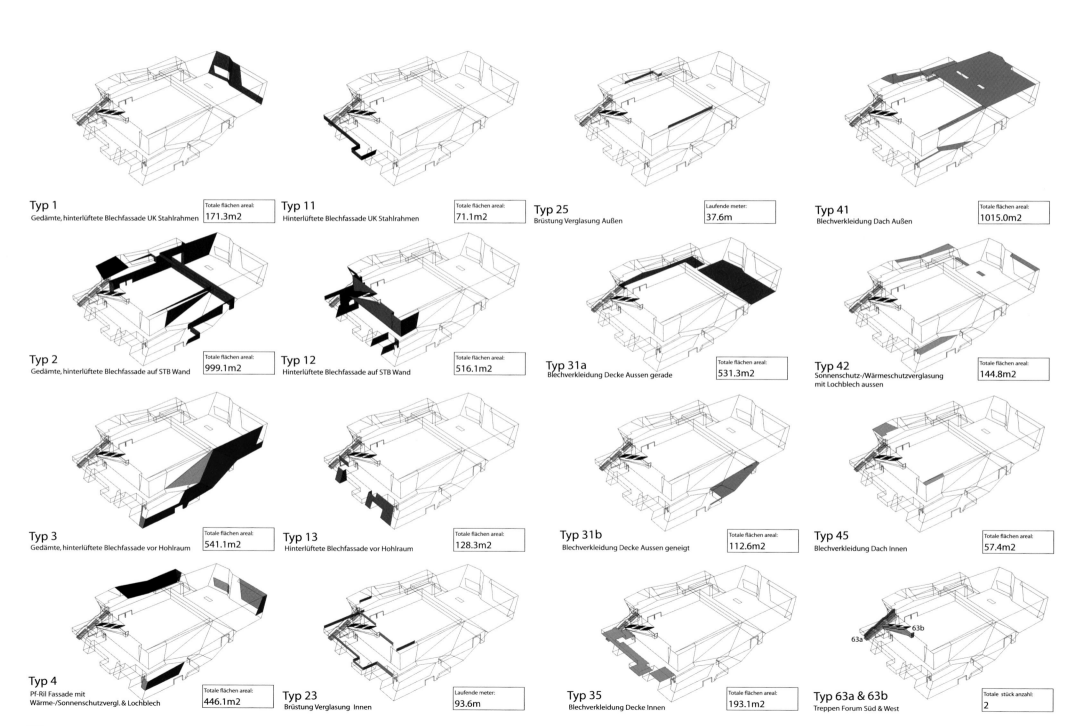

Typ 1
Gedämte, hinterlüftete Blechfassade UK Stahlrahmen

Totale flächen areal:
171.3m2

Typ 11
Hinterlüftete Blechfassade UK Stahlrahmen

Totale flächen areal:
71.1m2

Typ 25
Brüstung Verglasung Außen

Laufende meter:
37.6m

Typ 41
Blechverkleidung Dach Außen

Totale flächen areal:
1015.0m2

Typ 2
Gedämte, hinterlüftete Blechfassade auf STB Wand

Totale flächen areal:
999.1m2

Typ 12
Hinterlüftete Blechfassade auf STB Wand

Totale flächen areal:
516.1m2

Typ 31a
Blechverkleidung Decke Aussen gerade

Totale flächen areal:
531.3m2

Typ 42
Sonnenschutz-/Wärmeschutzverglasung
mit Lochblech aussen

Totale flächen areal:
144.8m2

Typ 3
Gedämte, hinterlüftete Blechfassade vor Hohlraum

Totale flächen areal:
541.1m2

Typ 13
Hinterlüftete Blechfassade vor Hohlraum

Totale flächen areal:
128.3m2

Typ 31b
Blechverkleidung Decke Aussen geneigt

Totale flächen areal:
112.6m2

Typ 45
Blechverkleidung Dach Innen

Totale flächen areal:
57.4m2

Typ 4
Pf-Ril Fassade mit
Wärme-/Sonnenschutzvergl. & Lochblech

Totale flächen areal:
446.1m2

Typ 23
Brüstung Verglasung Innen

Laufende meter:
93.6m

Typ 35
Blechverkleidung Decke Innen

Totale flächen areal:
193.1m2

Typ 63a & 63b
Treppen Forum Süd & West

Totale stück anzahl:
2

Illustration of the various facade types using the Forum

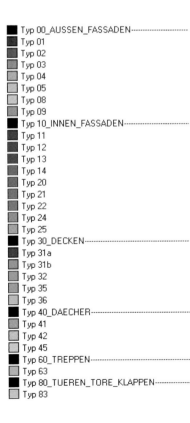
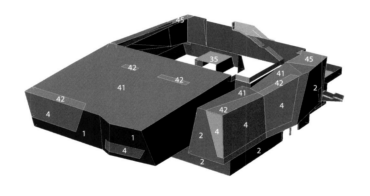

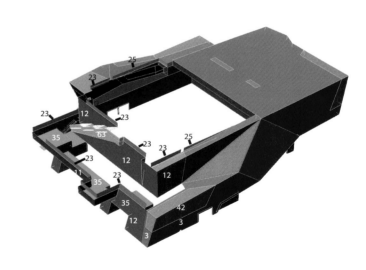

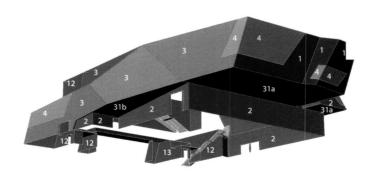

Development of the stainless-steel panels on the Forum

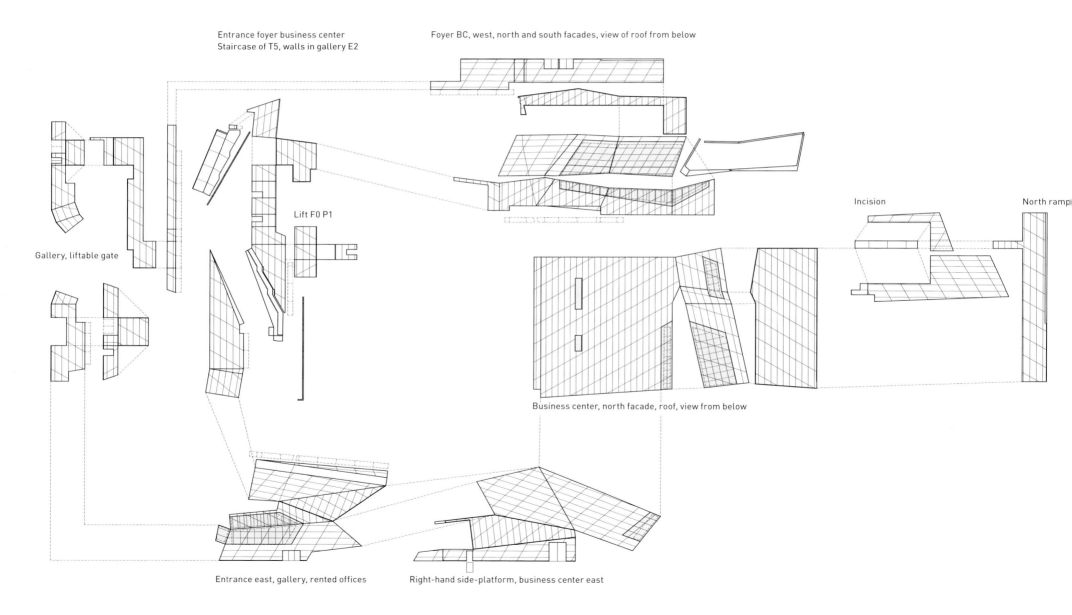

Entrance foyer business center
Staircase of T5, walls in gallery E2

Foyer BC, west, north and south facades, view of roof from below

Lift F0 P1

Gallery, liftable gate

Incision

North ramp

Business center, north facade, roof, view from below

Entrance east, gallery, rented offices

Right-hand side-platform, business center east

04.10.2007

04.09.2007

195

View from south: Forum
View from east: Forum

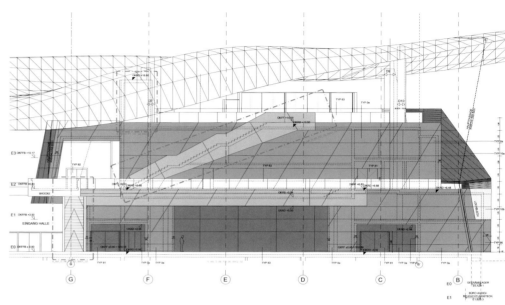

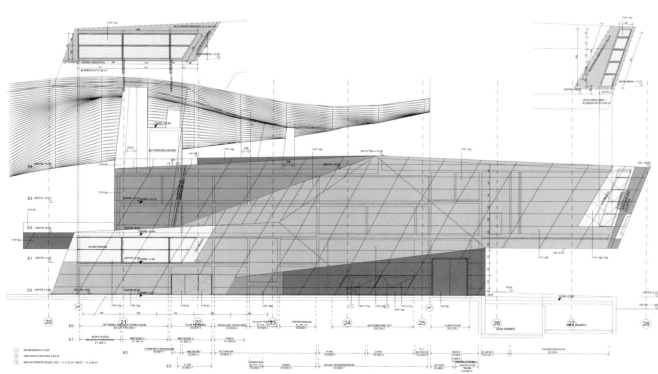

View from north: Forum
View from west: Forum

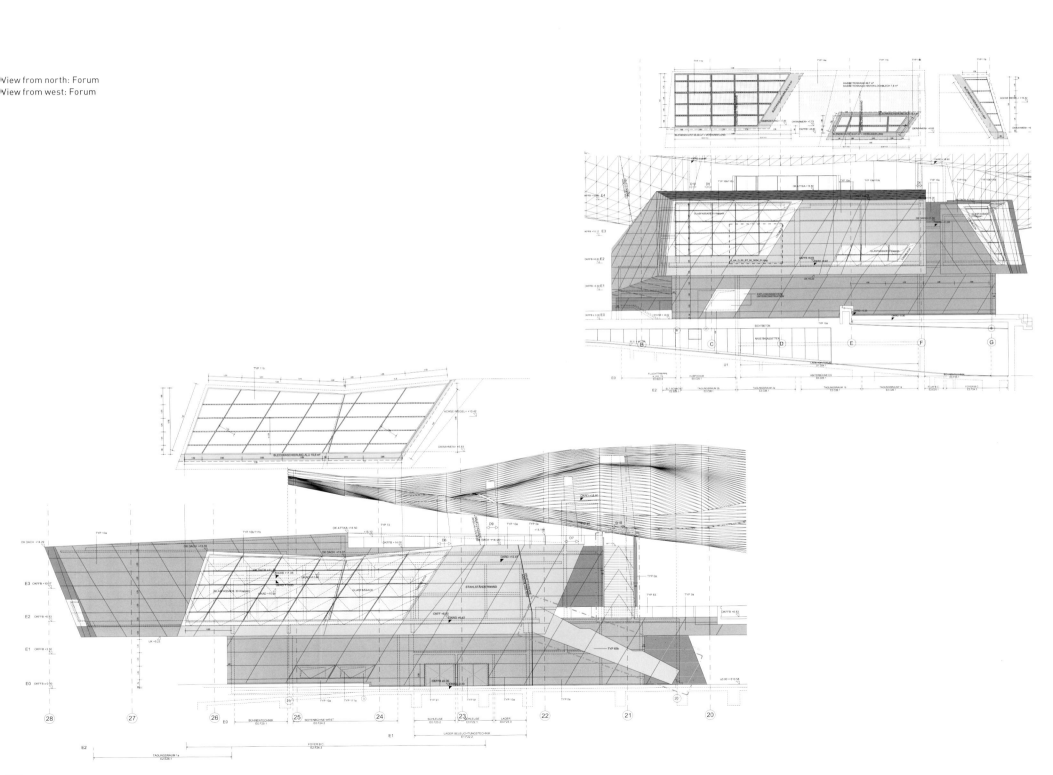

Detail of Forum

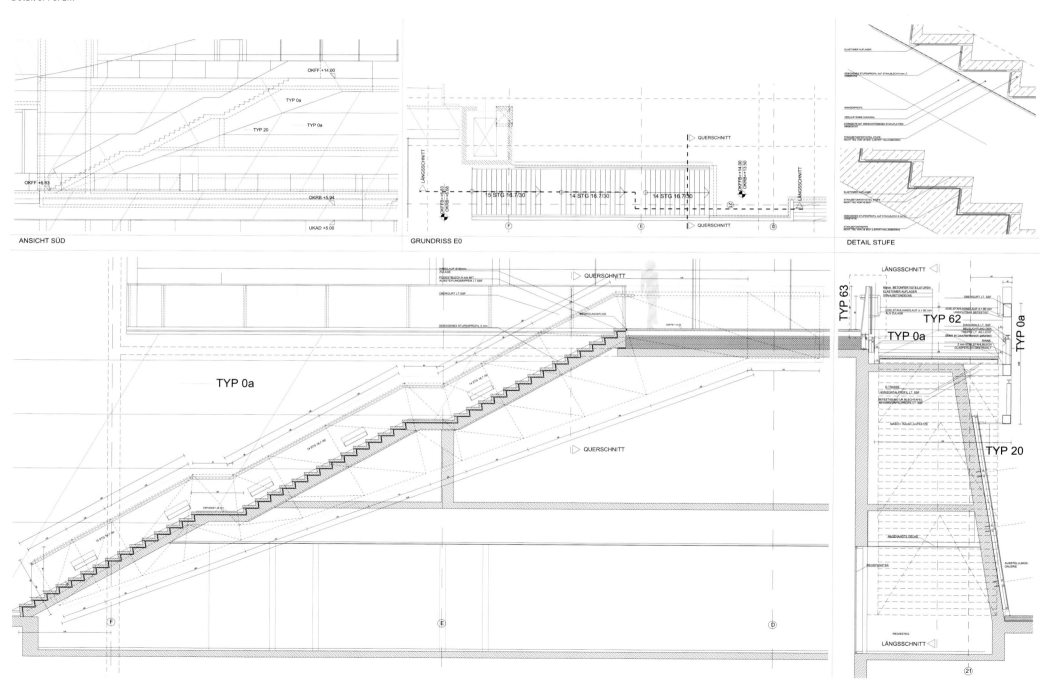

ANSICHT SÜD

GRUNDRISS E0

DETAIL STUFE

TYP 0a

TYP 20

TYP 0a

OKFF +14,00

OKFF +6,83

OKRB +5,94

UKAD +5,00

15 STG 16,7/30   14 STG 16,7/30   14 STG 16,7/30

QUERSCHNITT

LÄNGSSCHNITT

QUERSCHNITT

QUERSCHNITT

TYP 63

TYP 62

TYP 0a

TYP 0a

TYP 20

LÄNGSSCHNITT

LÄNGSSCHNITT

24.05.2007

18.05.2007

Detail sections of Forum/Business Center

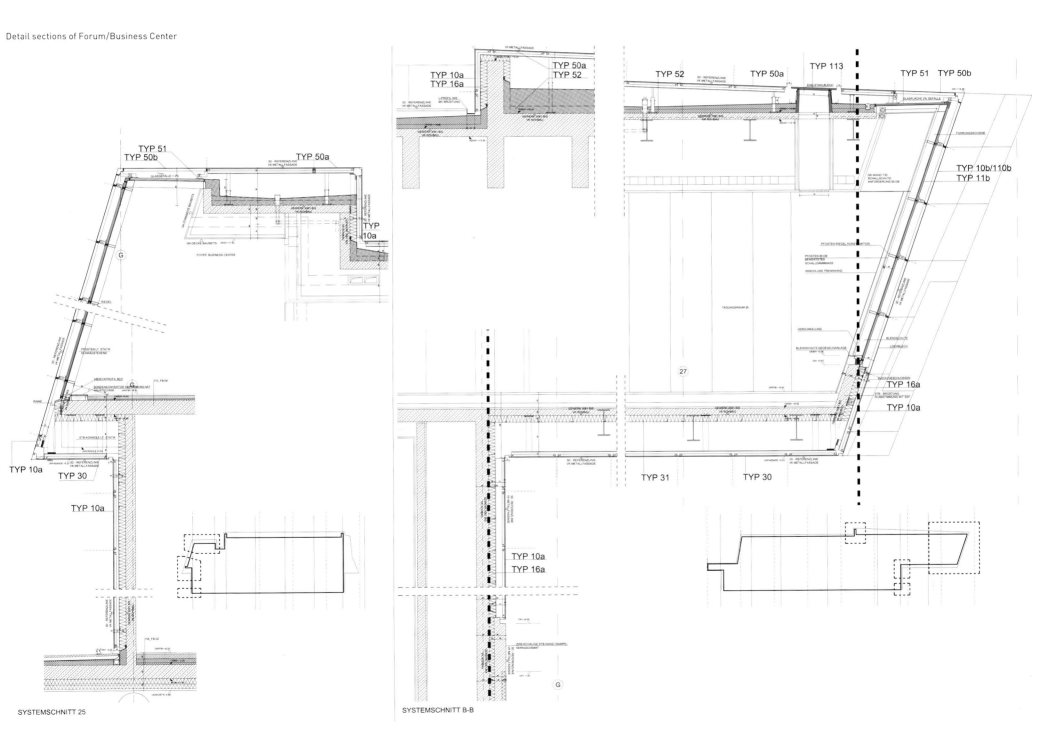

TYP 51
TYP 50b

TYP 50a

TYP 10a

TYP 10a

TYP 30

TYP 10a

SYSTEMSCHNITT 25

TYP 10a
TYP 16a

TYP 50a
TYP 52

TYP 52   TYP 50a   TYP 113   TYP 51   TYP 50b

TYP 10b/110b
TYP 11b

TYP 16a

TYP 10a

TYP 31   TYP 30

TYP 10a
TYP 16a

SYSTEMSCHNITT B-B

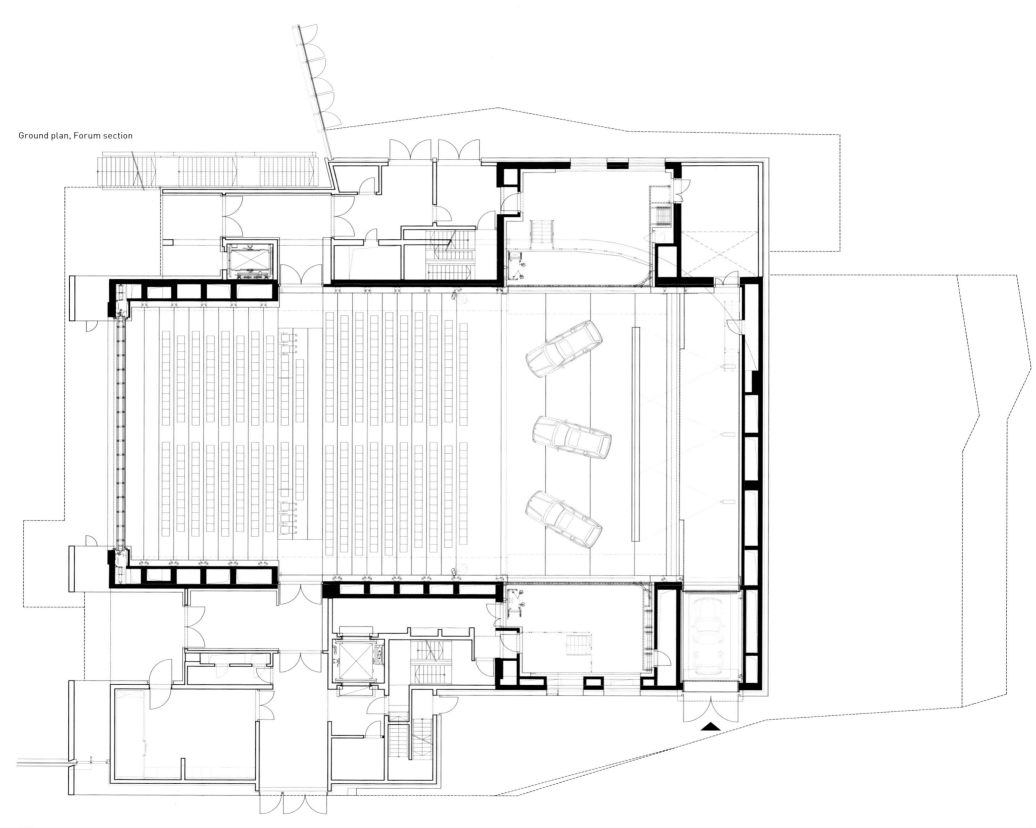

Ground plan, Forum section

29.05.2006

203

Classical theater

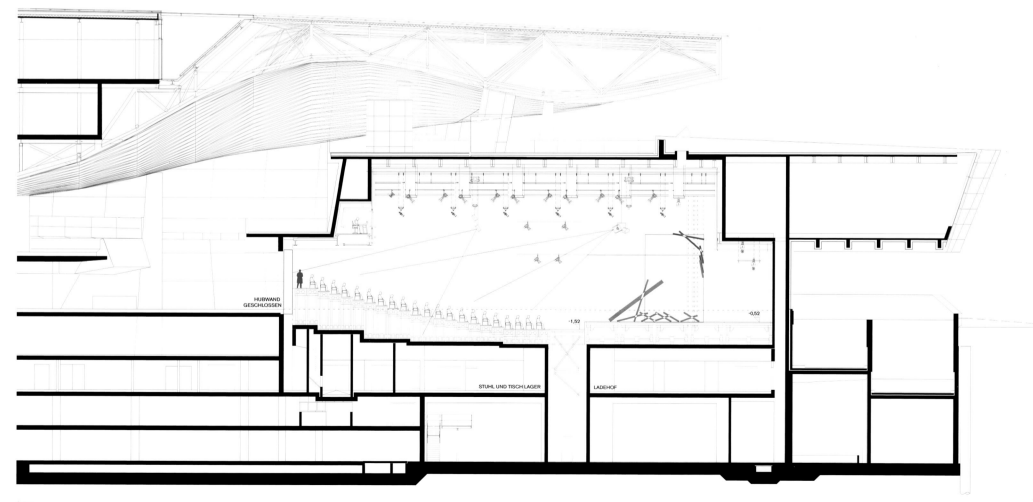

HUBWAND
GESCHLOSSEN

-1,52

-0,52

STUHL UND TISCH LAGER   LADEHOF

Depiction of the various hall topographies:
Left: Parliamentary seating, "balance-sheet press conference"
Right: Vehicle presentation
Bottom left: Horizontal floor "exhibition"
Bottom right: Cinema seating

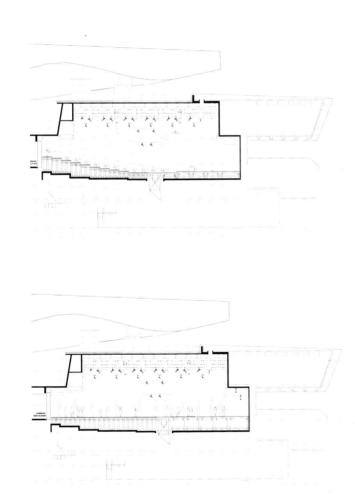

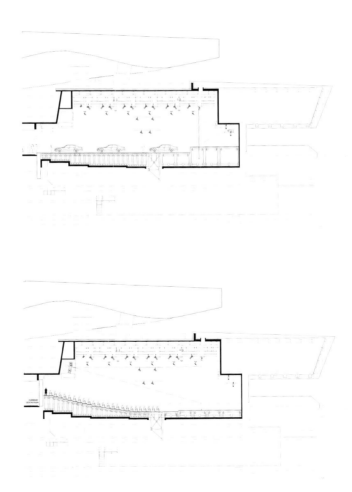

roggermaier
089/90 50 060

04.09.2007

7

The mushroom-shaped Tower in the southwest part of the Hall houses mixed uses, both publicly accessible ones such as shops, the Junior Campus children's & youth adventure areas, restaurants on several levels, as well as the private administrative area. Encapsulated interior spaces with walk-through terraces and open galleries form an abstract topography under the roof. In terms of construction, this Tower takes on a major role in the reinforcement and load-bearing work for the entire roof. The Tower core with its rectangular cross-section projects over the Hall approx. 10.5 meters on Levels E3 and E4 on the east side, approx. 4.0 or 6.0 meters on the other sides. In order to minimize the stresses on the cantilevered wall panels, the floor slabs in these areas are executed in a steel composite. The horizontal and vertical roof loads are supported on the south and west sides (cantilever of 6.0 meters).

Due to these stresses and the necessary warping limitations for the entire roof system, the cantilevered walls are prestressed. The rectangular core cross-section could not be carried out due to the delivery function on the first lower level. This meant that approx. 50% of the reinforcing core walls had to be taken up on Level E0. This was done by extending one core wall on Level E0 up to a supporting structural component. In order to model this load-bearing effect, the entire Tower was studied in a three-dimensional calculation using the finite elements method.

Axonometric view of the bearing structure in the Tower section

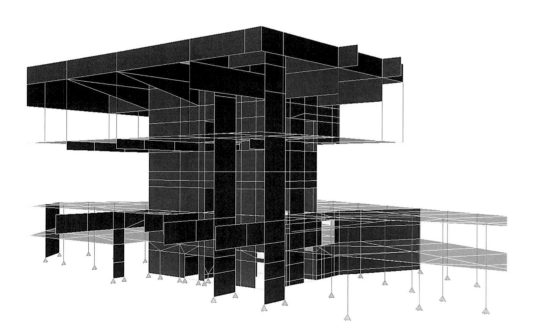
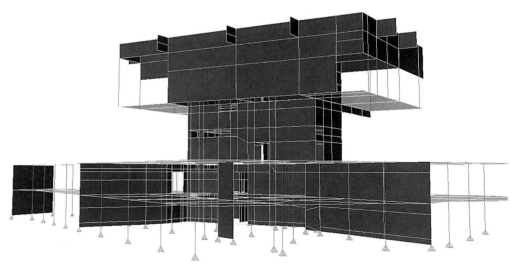

12.04.2006

Axonometric depiction of the stainless-steel cladding on the Tower

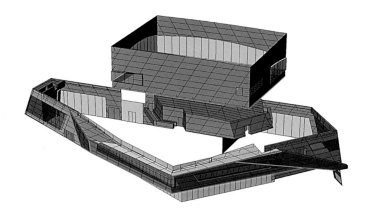

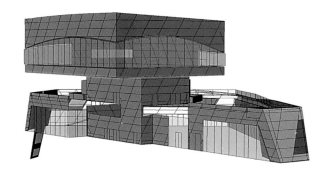

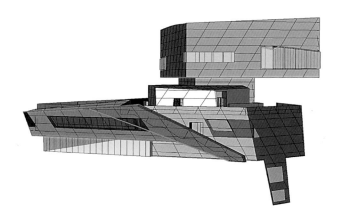

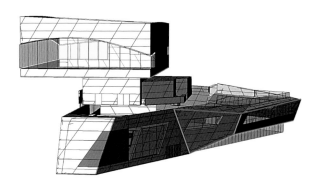

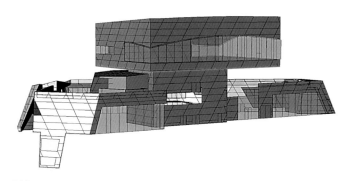

213

10.05.2006

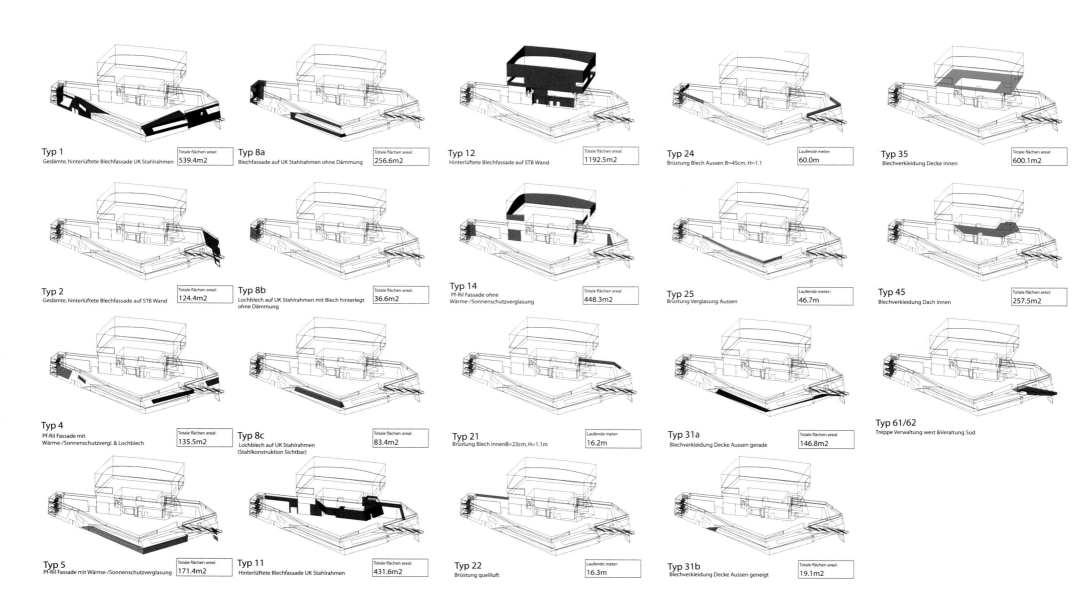

Typ 1
Gedämte, hinterlüftete Blechfassade UK Stahlrahmen

Totale flächen areal:
539.4m2

Typ 8a
Blechfassade auf UK Stahlrahmen ohne Dämmung

Totale flächen areal:
256.6m2

Typ 12
Hinterlüftete Blechfassade auf STB Wand

Totale flächen areal:
1192.5m2

Typ 24
Brüstung Blech Aussen B=45cm, H=1.1

Laufende meter:
60.0m

Typ 35
Blechverkleidung Decke Innen

Totale flächen areal:
600.1m2

Typ 2
Gedämte, hinterlüftete Blechfassade auf STB Wand

Totale flächen areal:
124.4m2

Typ 8b
Lochblech auf UK Stahlrahmen mit Blech hinterlegt ohne Dämmung

Totale flächen areal:
36.6m2

Typ 14
Pf-Ril Fassade ohne Wärme-/Sonnenschutzverglasung

Totale flächen areal:
448.3m2

Typ 25
Brüstung Verglasung Aussen

Laufende meter:
46.7m

Typ 45
Blechverkleidung Dach Innen

Totale flächen areal:
257.5m2

Typ 4
Pf-Ril Fassade mit Wärme-/Sonnenschutzvergl. & Lochblech

Totale flächen areal:
135.5m2

Typ 8c
Lochblech auf UK Stahlrahmen (Stahlkonstruktion Sichtbar)

Totale flächen areal:
83.4m2

Typ 21
Brüstung Blech InnenB=23cm, H=1.1m

Laufende meter:
16.2m

Typ 31a
Blechverkleidung Decke Aussen gerade

Totale flächen areal:
146.8m2

Typ 61/62
Treppe Verwaltung west &Veraltung Süd

Typ 5
Pf-Ril Fassade mit Wärme-/Sonnenschutzverglasung

Totale flächen areal:
171.4m2

Typ 11
Hinterlüftete Blechfassade UK Stahlrahmen

Totale flächen areal:
431.6m2

Typ 22
Brüstung quellluft

Laufende meter:
16.3m

Typ 31b
Blechverkleidung Decke Aussen geneigt

Totale flächen areal:
19.1m2

Depiction of the different facade types in the Tower section

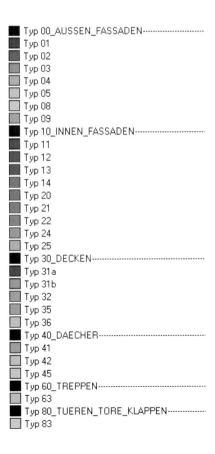

■ Typ 00_AUSSEN_FASSADEN-----------------------
■ Typ 01
■ Typ 02
□ Typ 03
□ Typ 04
□ Typ 05
□ Typ 08
□ Typ 09
■ Typ 10_INNEN_FASSADEN-------------------------
■ Typ 11
■ Typ 12
■ Typ 13
□ Typ 14
□ Typ 20
□ Typ 21
□ Typ 22
□ Typ 24
□ Typ 25
■ Typ 30_DECKEN--------------------------------------
■ Typ 31a
□ Typ 31b
□ Typ 32
□ Typ 35
□ Typ 36
■ Typ 40_DAECHER------------------------------------
□ Typ 41
□ Typ 42
□ Typ 45
■ Typ 60_TREPPEN-------------------------------------
□ Typ 63
■ Typ 80_TUEREN_TORE_KLAPPEN--------------
□ Typ 83

10.11.2006

Illustration of the various glazing types in the Restaurant area
as basis for the call for bids

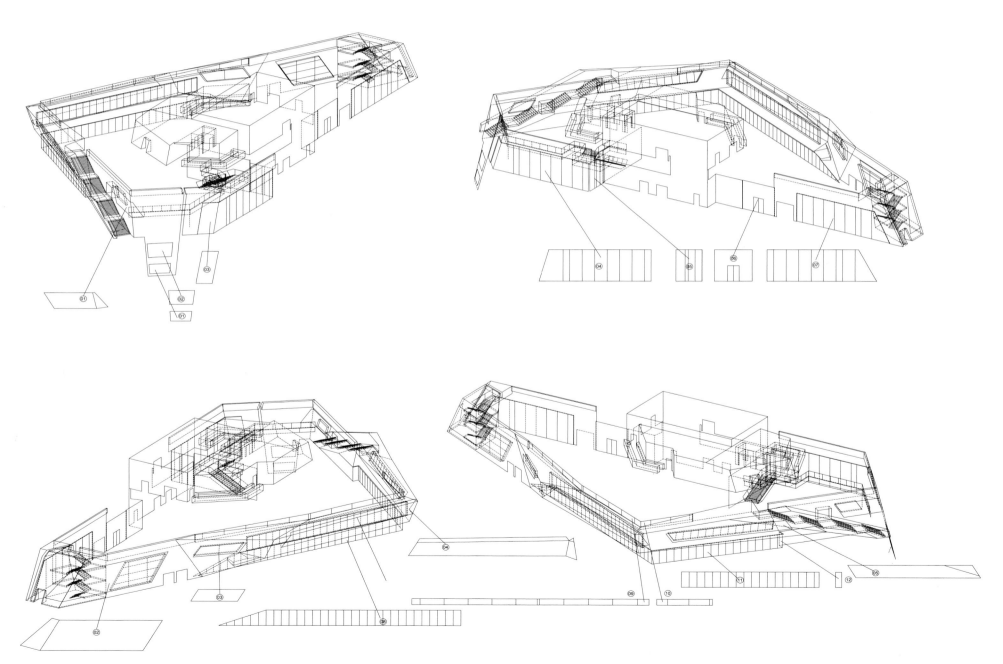

09.09.2005

Tower aspect

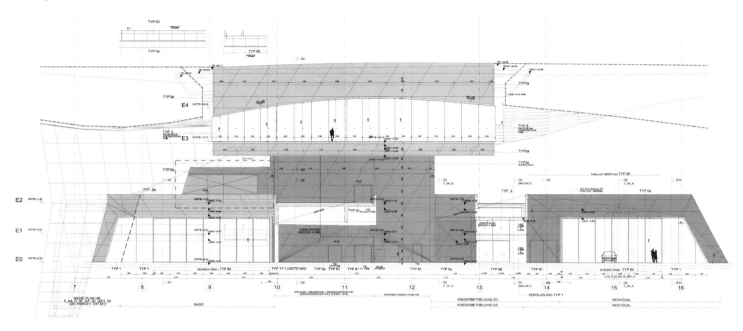

North-east aspect

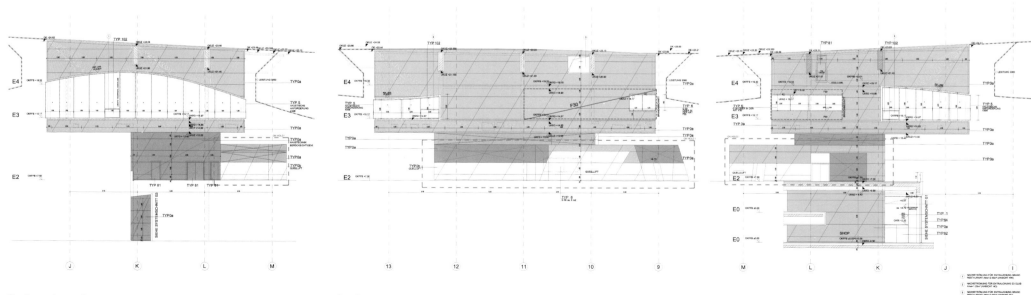

North-west aspect

South-west aspect

North-east aspect

South aspect, Tower section
West aspect

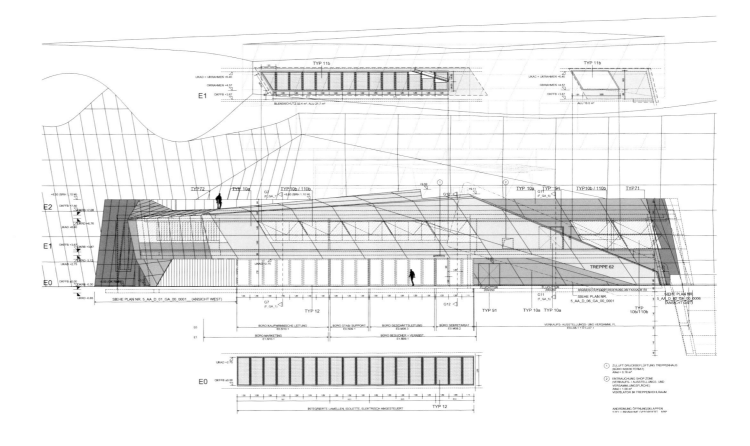

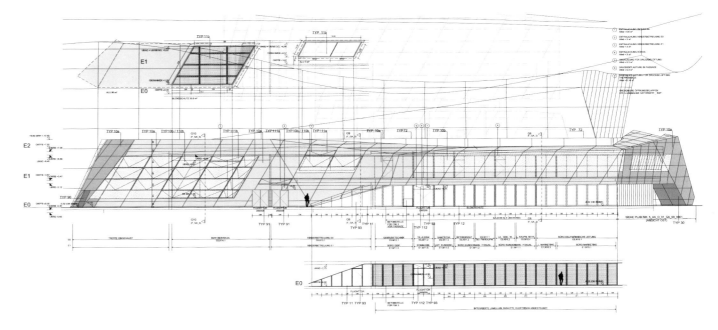

The stage for handing over new vehicles is called "Premiere." It is the final and most important station in the sequential process in which customer and vehicle are brought together. This realm is made up of the actual handing-over area with its 20 rotating platforms and 10 additional hand-over sites on the eastern facade, the actual exit ramp, and the Marina, a slightly raised area that cannot be driven on, located within the elliptically arranged rotating platforms and connected to the Lounge Level E3 via a 30-meter-long hanging stairway. The optimal presentation of the vehicles, together with the role played by specially dramatized sight lines in the "stage setting" as well as the uniqueness of the location, are designed to make vehicle delivery an authentic and one-of-a-kind experience for the customer.

The rotating platforms not only ensure that the vehicle is always presented to the customer from its "best side," but can also be turned for entry and exit to ensure a minimum of maneuvering. The hand-over spots are lit with HMI lamps. These are integrated into the ceiling inside lightproof boxes of approx. 6 meters in length. Flexible blades on the underside of the light boxes shield the direct view of the lamps and minimize the light reflections on the car paint. Rotating platforms and lighting can be synchronized via PDA by the customer service representative directly on site, individually for every hand-over spot, creating pre-set scenes that can be called up at will. The air exchange of approx. 60,000 cubic meters per hour required in this area had to be accomplished through the floor due to the otherwise natural ventilation in the Hall. The entire area is equipped with a hollow floor with a high-pressure exhaust function, making it possible to draw off the vehicle emissions as close as possible to the point of origin. The efficiency of the position and design of the intake and outflow openings was simulated and optimized three-dimensionally in elaborate CFD calculations.

In this section of the building, too, all technical services were integrated behind a sculpturally formed stainless steel cover. Because of the special geometry of the tilted parapets atop the elliptical floor plan and the trapeze-shaped panel sections, 3-millimeter-thick metal sheets in some cases needed to be made with up to 3 different radii per sheet. The attachment of the panels to the rib-like sub-structure, similar to shipbuilding, was accomplished without visible screws by way of bolts shot into the rear sides of the panels.

17.04.2005

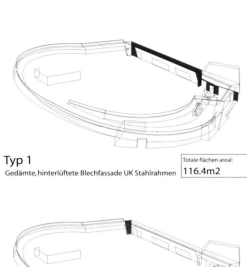

Typ 1
Gedämte, hinterlüftete Blechfassade UK Stahlrahmen

Totale flächen areal:
116.4m2

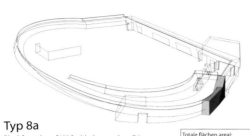

Typ 8a
Blechfassade auf UK Stahlrahmen ohne Dämmung

Totale flächen areal:
96.8m2

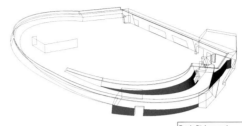

Typ 13
Hinterlüftete Blechfassade vor Hohlraum

Totale flächen areal:
148.0m2

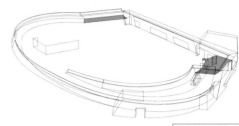

Typ 35
Blechverkleidung Decke Innen

Totale flächen areal:
160.9m2

Typ 2
Gedämte, hinterlüftete Blechfassade auf STB Wand

Totale flächen areal:_
35.8m2

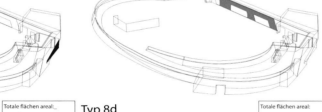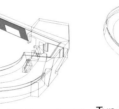

Typ 8d
Lochblech vor Dømmung

Totale flächen areal:
86.8m2

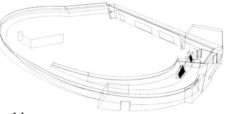

Typ 14
Pf-Ril Fassade ohne
Wärme-/Sonnenschutzverglasung

Totale flächen areal:
17.8m2

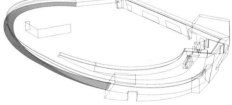

Typ 36
Blechverkleidung Decke Innen gekrümmt

Totale flächen areal:
308.6m2

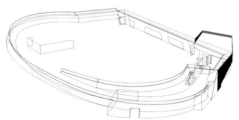

Typ 3
Gedämte, hinterlüftete Blechfassade vor Hohlraum

Totale flächen areal:
98.8m2

Typ 11
Hinterlüftete Blechfassade UK Stahlrahmen

Totale flächen areal:
74.8m2

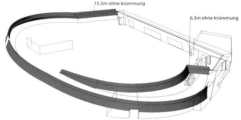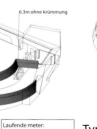

15.5m ohne krümmung

6.3m ohne krümmung

Typ 20
Brüstung Premiere (1-dimensional gekrümmt)

Laufende meter:
197.1m (788.8m2 fläche)

Typ 41
Blechverkleidung Dach Außen

Totale flächen areal:
300.9m2

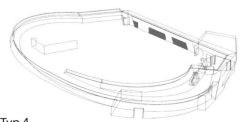

Typ 4
Pf-Ril Fassade mit
Wärme-/Sonnenschutzvergl. & Lochblech

Totale flächen areal:
43.9m2

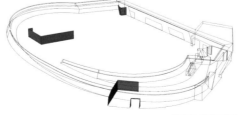

Typ 12
Hinterlüftete Blechfassade auf STB Wand

Totale flächen areal:
128.4m2

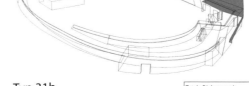

Typ 31b
Blechverkleidung Decke Aussen geneigt

Totale flächen areal:
151.6m2

228

Depiction of facade types in Premiere section

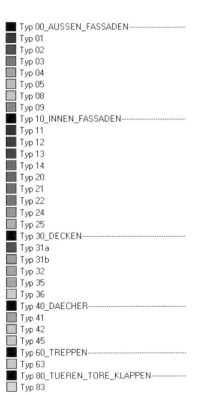

Typ 00_AUSSEN_FASSADEN
Typ 01
Typ 02
Typ 03
Typ 04
Typ 05
Typ 08
Typ 09
Typ 10_INNEN_FASSADEN
Typ 11
Typ 12
Typ 13
Typ 14
Typ 20
Typ 21
Typ 22
Typ 24
Typ 25
Typ 30_DECKEN
Typ 31a
Typ 31b
Typ 32
Typ 35
Typ 36
Typ 40_DAECHER
Typ 41
Typ 42
Typ 45
Typ 60_TREPPEN
Typ 63
Typ 80_TUEREN_TORE_KLAPPEN
Typ 83

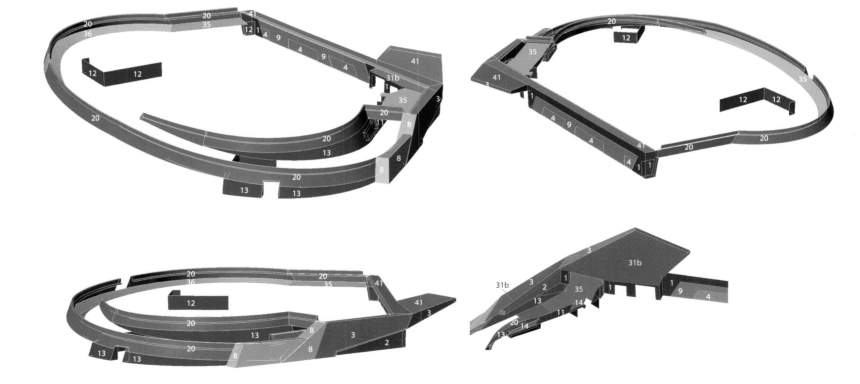

Ground plan, Premiere

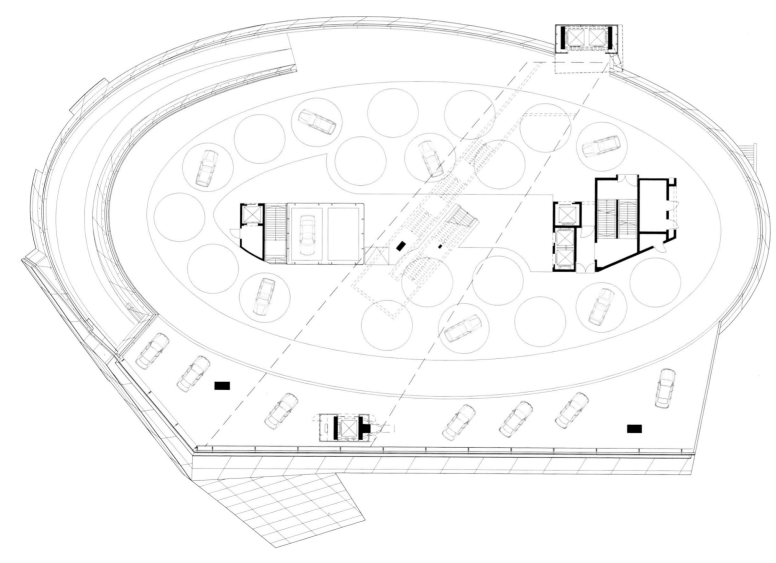

Development of the stainless steel panels in the Premiere

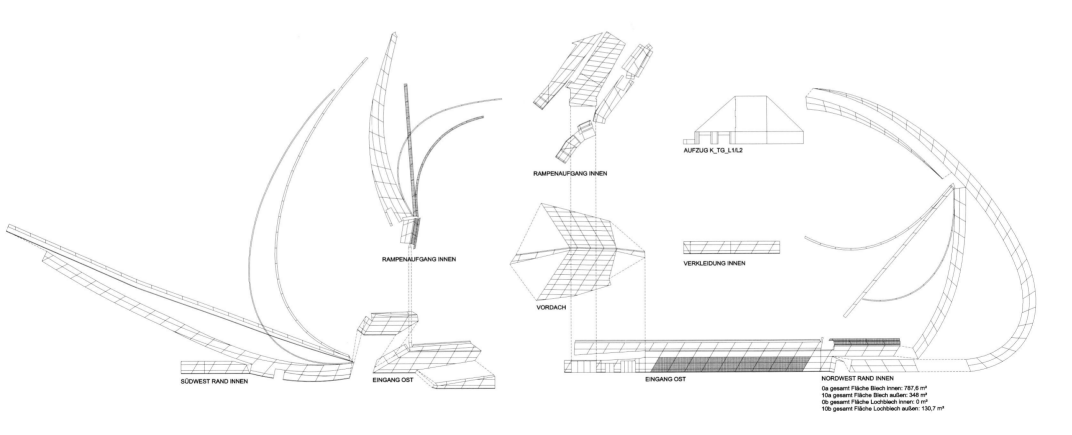

RAMPENAUFGANG INNEN

AUFZUG K_TG_L1/L2

RAMPENAUFGANG INNEN

VERKLEIDUNG INNEN

VORDACH

SÜDWEST RAND INNEN

EINGANG OST

EINGANG OST

NORDWEST RAND INNEN
0a gesamt Fläche Blech innen: 787,6 m²
10a gesamt Fläche Blech außen: 348 m²
0b gesamt Fläche Lochblech innen: 0 m²
10b gesamt Fläche Lochblech außen: 130,7 m²

South-east aspect
East aspect

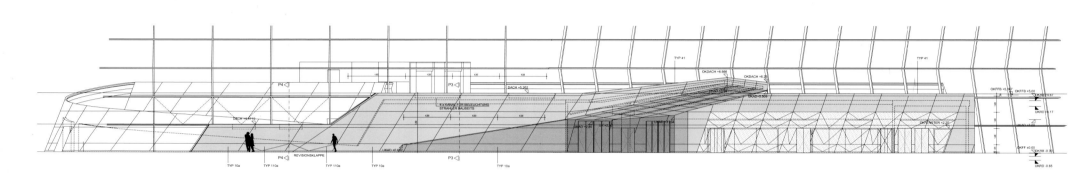

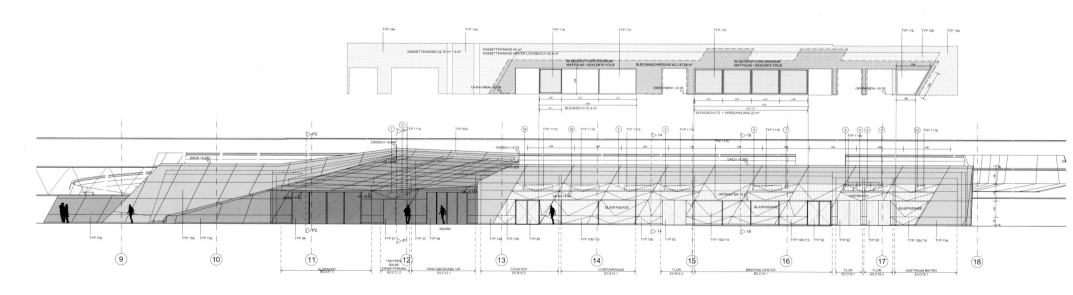

04.09.2007

234

04.09.2007

Detail sections, Premiere

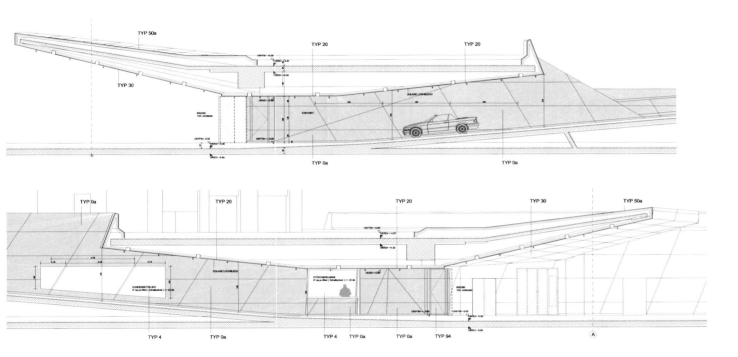

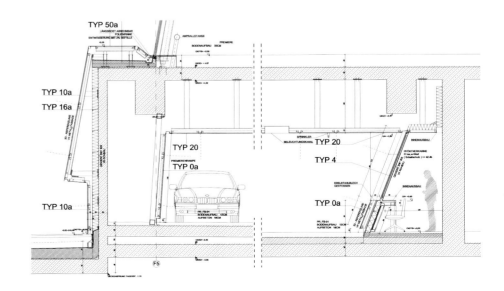

Premiere platform, total V-section through descent ramp

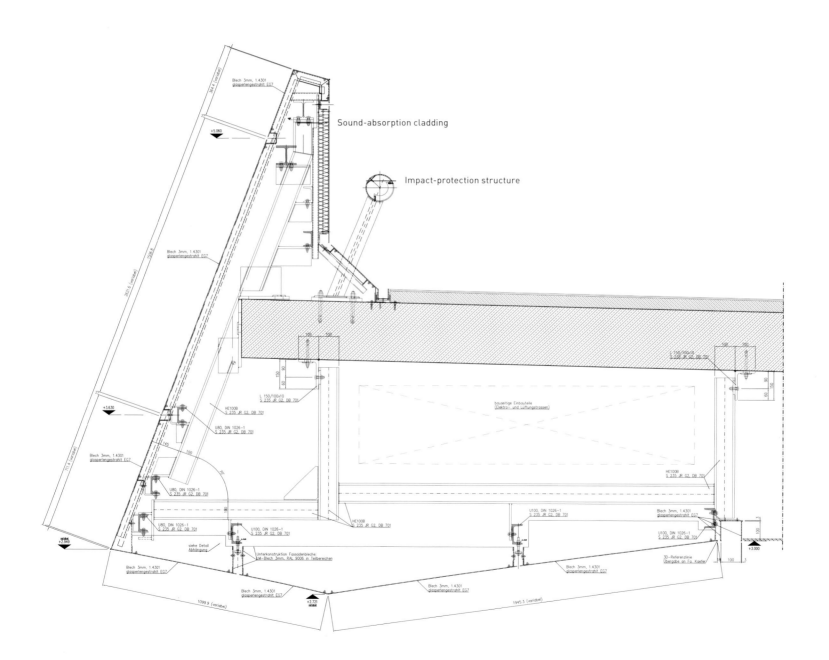

Sound-absorption cladding

Impact-protection structure

18.05.2007

04.09.2007

Appendix

BMW WELT, MUNICH, GERMANY (2001–2007)

Client BMW AG, Munich, Germany
Design and Planning Coop Himmelb(l)au
Wolf D. Prix / W. Dreibholz & Partner ZT GmbH
Principal in Charge Wolf D. Prix
Project Architect Paul Kath
Design Team Wolf D. Prix, Tom Wiscombe, Paul Kath,
Waltraut Hoheneder, Mona Marbach
Partial Project Architects Günther Weber, Penelope Rüttimann,
Renate Weissenböck, Verena Perius, Mona Marbach

Project Team Hans Aescht, Beatrix Basting, Guy Bebiè, Chris Beccone, Johannes
Behrens, Marcelo Bernardi, Pawel Bodzak, Verena Boyer, Antja Bulthaup, Timo
Carl, Jan Chaldil, Ing Tse Chen, Tadeusz Chimiak, Andrea Christmann, Patrick
Erhardt, Stephan Exsternbrink, Wolfgang Fiel, Benedikt Frass, Helmut Frötscher,
Volker Gessendorfer, Andrea Graser, Lukas Haller, Markus Henning, Armin Hess,
Jens Hoff, Tamas Horvath, Robert Huebser, Astrid Jagersberger, Marin Jurycz,
Gregor Kassl, Areta Keller, Markus Klausecker, Tobias Klein, Martin Konrad,
Quirin Krumbholz, Caroline Kufferath, Marion Lattenmayer, Stefan Laub, Wolfgang
Leitgeb, Andreas Mieling, Karin Miesenberger, Dennis Milam, Elke Müller, Henrike
Münker, Claudia Nehammer, Martin Oberascher, Alexander Ott, Stefan Pfefferle,
Florian Pfeifer, Markus Pillhofer, Ekkehard Rehfeld, Goswin Rothenthal, Wolfgang
Ruthensteiner, Jasmin Sauerbier, Florian Schafschetzy, Kristina Schinegger,
Karolin Schmidbaur, Patrick Schneider, Katharina Schneider, Hubert Schoba,
Angus Schoenberger, Andrea Schöning, Anja Sorger, Gernot Stangl, Mark
Steinmetz, Sigrid Steinwender, Martina Tippelskirch, Dionicio Valdez, Pascal
Vauclair, Akvile Rimantaite, Andreas Weissenbach, Heribert Wolfmayer, Irina Zahler
Supported by Paul Biernat, Caroline Ecker, Gesine Görlich, Christian Halm, Anna
Illenseer, Cynthia Kallmeyer Matt Kirkham, Petra Königsegger, Susanne Leeb,
Emilia Margaretha, Isabelle Ost, Angelika Pöschl, Heidelinde Resch, Timo Rieke

Project Management in-house Hans Lechner ZT GmbH, Vienna, Austria
Project Director: Sabine Liebenau
Hans Lechner, Sabine Liebenau, Babette Schwarz, Susanne Danzmeyer
Beyrl, Sabine Ebster, Michael Scherz, Nina Wohlrab, Herbert Kanov,
Christian Ellmeier, Horst Fuchs, Dietmar Gobitzer, Andreas Haiderer,
Daniela Zupan, Andreas Wintersteiner, Nina Truttmann, Elfriede Tösch,
Christian Szeglat, Michaela Summer, Jan Schubert, Martina Roj, Christina
Moder Borsic, Walter Kräutler, Emanuel Krause, Tatiana Hergarden
Construction Documents Roof and Facade: Coop Himmelb(l)au, Vienna, Austria
Project Director: Günther Weber
Construction Documents Concrete Works, Interior Fittings, Tender,
Construction Administration: Schmitt, Stumpf, Frühauf + Partner, Munich, Germany
Project Directors: Manfred Rudolf, Ferdinand Tremmel
Viktor Schmitt, Ferdinand Tremmel, Manfred Rudolf, Achim Grünig, Matthias
Lettau, Christian Hertneck, Frank Haake, Thomas Wolf, Manfred Pietsch, Andreas
Höregott, Ernst Wander, Florian Böck, Christian Höregott, Thomas Wolf, Ernst
Wander, Rainer Linhardt, Manfred Pietsch, Rolf Koppermann, Hans Reder,
Helmar Hüning, Anna Levitas, Dieter Benetzeder, Bernd Gschwender, Ulrich
Kauer, Appolonia Lorenz, Helmut Metzler, Holger Schwarz, Miklos Tövissy, Rainer
Tielke, Judith Reisert, Daniela Ried, Arne Rucks, Thomas Götzinger, Thomas Abt,
Benedikt Kronenbitter, Simone Mank, Kerstin Riebeck, Felix Singer, Ingrid Scippa
Structural Engineering B+G Ingenieure, Bollinger und Grohmann GmbH,
Frankfurt, Germany
Project Director: Jörg Schneider
Klaus Bollinger, Manfred Grohmann, Jörg Schneider, Michael Wagner, Matthias
Witte, Daniel Pfanner, Fr. Simon, Alexander Berger, Richard Troelenberg, Jürgen
Aßmus, Hr. Wermischer
Schmitt, Stumpf, Frühauf + Partner, Munich, Germany
Project Director: Ferdinand Tremmel
Mechanical Engineering (HVACS) Kühn Bauer + Partner, Munich, Germany
Project Director: Günther Hammitzsch
Michael Kühn sen., Michael Kühn jun., Erika Kühn, Werner Bauer, Günther
Hammitzsch, Jörg Mundle, Richard Sagner, Jochen Bergmeier, Gerhard Jülich,
Nils Brandstätter, Jochen Manger, Katrin Wötzel, Michael Brach, Petra Brunk,
Ulrike Ibbach
Electrical System and Lifts PRO Elektroplan, Ottobrunn, Germany
Project Director: Robert Rapp
Bernd Ropeter jun., Robert Rapp, Bernd Lohmann, Josef Emmer, Johannes
Heuwieser, Alexandra Weber, Angelika Kahnt, Peter Feike, Luzia Ho, Karl Heinz
May, Markus Bauer, Dorothea Kuzora, Petra Hartmann, Christine Müller

Lighting Consultant AG-Licht, Bonn, Germany
Wilfried Kramb, Klaus Adolph, Michaela Kruse
Building Physics Büro Dr. Pfeiler, Graz, Austria
Wolfgang Gollner, Sybill Kerschbaumer
Facade Consultant Emmer Pfenninger + Partner AG, Münchenstein, Switzerland
Emmer Pfenninger, Pierre Scherrer
R + R Fuchs, Munich, Germany
Richard Fuchs
Stage Consultant Theater Projekte Daberto + Kollegen, Munich, Germany
Project Director: Frank Schöpf
Reinhold Daberto, Frank Schöpf, Sebastian Fenk, Ulrich Zimmermann, Jörg Lilleike,
Jochen Bauch, Benito Serravalle, Tom Smith, Ralph Preller, Markus Pusch
Photovoltaic Plant (PV Plant) Transsolar, Klima Engineering, Stuttgart, Germany
Stefan Holst, Siegfried Baumgartner
Kitchen Technology PBB Planungsbüro Balke, Munich, Germany
Elisabeth Balke, Joachim Billinger, Manuela Kojcinovic, Gerhard Holler
Landscape Design realgruen Landschaftsarchitekten, Munich, Germany
Wolf Dieter Auch, Klaus D. Neumann, Eva Prasch, Stefan Huber
Fire Protection Kersken & Kirchner, Munich, Germany
Marita Kersken-Kirchner, Thilo Hoffmann, Susann Jurisch
Height Elevation Access TAW Weisse, Hamburg, Germany
Thomas Weisse
Traffic Engineering Lang & Burkhardt, Munich, Germany
Michael Angelsberger
Civil Engineering, Road Construction Ingenieurbüro Schoenenberg,
Munich, Germany
Rüdiger Schönenberg, Jiri Wesely
Orientation Systems Büro für Gestaltung / Wangler & Abele, Munich, Germany
Ursula Wangler, Frank Abele, Andreas Egensperger, Silvia Gagalick
Inspection Engineer Zilch, Müller, Henneke, Munich, Germany
Dr. Andre Müller, Karl Schwindel, Nicolai Pfitzenmeier, Hr. Schemmann,
Yvonne Giese, Arnd Paus, Daniele Salvatore, Stefan Summerer, Peter Lenz,
Erwin Penka, Wolfgang Niedermeier

Project team and project structure

With the start of the project, i.e. the actual awarding of the contract to Coop Himmelb(l)au as general planner at the end of 2001, what were already high functional and design aspirations were compounded by an additional factor: coordination and documentation, duties of a scope that is not easy to pin down.

This kind of project, with more than one hundred persons directly involved on the part of the general planner and just as many planners at BMW AG, plus some 500 to 1,000 workers on the construction site (not counting the contractors' planning offices working in the background and the large number of manufacturers with their own employees) poses a singularly complex challenge. For example, if one were to lay out side-by-side all the correspondence exchanged (92,000 letters averaging 10 pages), the paper would cover the entire gross floor area of BMW Welt, or the entire plot plus half of the plant floor. The more than 100,000 plans that were drawn correspond to the area of almost 20 football fields. And all of these documents must be stored for 30 years!

Construction was carried out by way of individually awarded contracts, involving approximately 550 different trades or contracts. Data for all of these (for example, for 1,600 contact persons and 388 cost centers) had to be recorded and maintained.

Over 20,000 items were processed in various cost calculations, and 8,000 detailed quantity calculations were carried out.

112 calls for tender were issued by 8 different specialized planning teams, who then reviewed the bids under consideration of all of the framework specifications (with decisions being made in parallel to the construction work in progress) and prepared them for negotiation with BMW Purchasing. 4,400 cost change requests from 388 different contractors (as of June 2007; a total of 6,000 are expected by the end of the project) had to be reviewed, evaluated and processed. 1,000 individual and progress-payment invoices had been recorded, examined and forwarded for payment by June 2007 (2,500 are anticipated). Over 70,000 emails were written or distributed and over 100,000 plans (not including sketches) were reviewed.

Planning phase

180 architects and engineers for the execution, as well as 30 planning offices working under the General Planner 25,000 plans drawn up in DIN A0 size, corresponding to 2 tons of paper.

BUILDING

Site area approx. 25,000 m^2 (roughly equivalent to 3 football fields)

Total gross floor space approx. 73,000 m^2 (excluding ramps) = 100 %

Aboveground floor space approx. 28,500 m^2 = 40 %

Underground floor space approx. 44,500 m^2 = 60 %

Stories

Level –3: approx. – 13 m

Level –2: approx. – 10 m

Level –1: approx. – 7 m

Level 0: 0 m

Level 1: approx. + 5 / + 6,5 / + 7,5 m

Level 2: approx. + 15 m

Level 3: approx. + 19 m

Gross volume 531,000 m^3

Building 180 m long, 130 m wide, 30 m high

Competition (1st Prize) 2001

Start of planning November 2001

Start of construction August 2003

Opening 20/21 October 2007

Building costs above 100 Mio Euro

BUILDING SHELL

15,000 m² building pit, 210 m long and 120 m wide

Material excavated from pit 158,400 m³ (corresponds to approx. 12,000 truckloads)

Drilled piles 775 (17 m deep, Ø 88 cm) with a combined length of approx. 11,800 m

Visible area retaining wall approx. 5,147 m²

Visible area shear girder approx. 1,210 m²

Anchor total length approx. 11,458 m in 2 anchor layers

Building pit 14 m deep (8 m below groundwater level)

Steel rods 3.6 million m used, equal to almost one quarter the diameter of the earth

Concrete base plate waterproofed concrete approx. 19,500 m³

Concrete perimeter wall waterproofed concrete approx. 3,200 m³

Reinforcement total 8,500 t

Concrete total approx. 55,000 m³, equal to 6100 truckloads

Steel-reinforced concrete 9,000 t steel-reinforced concrete was used, including 3,000 t hand-laid steel rods

Steel 4,000 t steel used in the building, about one quarter of which in the Double Cone

Glass 14,500 m²

Stainless steel sheeting 10,000 m²

People up to 1,100 people worked at the building site simultaneously

ROOF STRUCTURE

16,000 m² roof area

26 assembly towers supported the roof during building. The roof was raised using hydraulic presses and finally brought to rest on the building's 11 columns.

Min. 8 cm: amount of movement in the roof caused by temperature fluctuations. These movements are taken up at the roof's edge by a crease in the facade. This crease acts like a spring, eliminating the need for movement joints, etc.

6,300 m² solar cell elements (3,660 panels) with an output of about 810 MWh per year

INTERIOR

Lamps approx. 15,000 lamps in the entire building

Cooling output 2,700 kW

Heating output 3,800 kW

Moving air when in operation 400,000 m³

Sprinkler heads 10,000 sprinkler heads to extinguish incipient fires

Rooms 1,200 doors lead to 1,154 rooms

Air firewall 120 m long: the air firewall in the Plaza

RESTAURANTS / SHOPS

Club Restaurant 50 seats, E3

Restaurant International 160 seats, E2, and 150 seats on the outside terrace

Bistro 80 seats, E0

Coffee Bar 20 seats, E2

BMW Shop with lifestyle and merchandizing articles 700 m²

OPERATIONS

Parking spaces around 600

Jobs approx. 200 new jobs

Car deliveries some 170 (max. 250) per day

People 45,000 people picking up cars per year, 95,000 people in all including accompanying guests

Visitors around 850,000 annually, 300,000 of them tourists

DOUBLE CONE

Height 28 m (BMW Museum 25 m, BMW Tower 104.5 m)

Diameter 45 m

Steel structure 820 t weight in the steel structure

Floor space 870 m² total floor space (ground floor: 450 m², basement: 420 m²)

Facade 900 different glass elements with an axial grid of 5.5 m were fabricated for the facade of the Double Cone. 2,850 m² facade area

Events max. 850 event guests

COOP HIMMELB(L)AU

Coop Himmelb(l)au was founded by Wolf D. Prix, Helmut Swiczinsky and Michael Holzer in Vienna, Austria in 1968, and is active in architecture, urban planning, design, and art. In 1988, a second studio was opened in Los Angeles, USA.

In 2000, Wolfdieter Dreibholz joined Coop Himmelb(l)au as CEO of Coop Himmelb(l)au Mex S. A. de C. V. and became a partner of Coop Himmelb(l)au Wolf D. Prix / W. Dreibholz & Partner ZT GmbH, becoming CEO in 2004. Michael Holzer left the team in 1971. Helmut Swiczinsky retired in 2002 from Coop Himmelb(l)au's daily operations and in 2006 from the office for health reasons. Since then the studio was run through Wolf D. Prix, Wolfdieter Dreibholz and Partners. Those are Karolin Schmidbaur, Paul Kath, Markus Pillhofer, Frank Stepper and Michael Volk.

Wolf D. Prix, born in Vienna in 1942, is a cofounder of Coop Himmelb(l)au. He studied architecture at the Vienna University of Technology, the Architectural Association of London, and the Southern California Institute of Architecture (SCI-Arc) in Los Angeles. Since 1993, Wolf D. Prix has been Professor for Head of the Institute for Architecture and serves as Vice-Rector of the university. He taught as a Visiting Professor at the Architectural Association in London in 1984 and at Harvard University in Cambridge, Massachusetts in 1990. From 1985 to 1995, Wolf D. Prix was active as Adjunct Professor at the SCI-Arc in Los Angeles. Since 1998, he has been a faculty member of Columbia University in New York. In 1999, Wolf D. Prix was awarded the Harvey S. Perloff Professorship at the University of California Los Angeles (UCLA). In 2001 he was made an Adjunct Professor at UCLA. Since 2001 he has been a Doctor Honoris Causa de la Universidad de Palermo, Buenos Aires, Argentina. In 2004, Wolf D. Prix received the Annie Spink Award for Excellence in Architectural Education for his commitment to teaching and training. From 1995 to 1997, Wolf D. Prix was a member of the architectural committee in the Austrian Federal Ministry of Science, Research, and the Arts. He is a member of the Austrian Art Senate as well as of the European Academy of Sciences and Arts. Furthermore, Wolf D. Prix is a member of the Architectural Association Austria, Union of German Architects (BDA) in Germany, the Architectural Union Santa Clara in Cuba, the Royal Institute of British Architects (RIBA), the American Institute of Architects (AIA) and the Architectural Association Italy. In 2006, he was the commissioner for the Austrian contribution for the Tenth International Architecture Biennale in Venice.

Wolfdieter Dreibholz was born in Vienna in 1941. He trained at the Technical University of Vienna, graduating in 1966 as a Dipl. Ing. with an engineering degree in architecture.

From 1968 to 1974 he worked as an assistant at the Faculty of Architecture at the Graz University of Technology. He graduated from there in 1977 as Doctor of Technical Sciences. From 1978 to 1998 Wolfdieter Dreibholz worked with the Planning Department of the federal state of Styria. He was appointed Director in 1990. In this capacity he was responsible for all public building projects, including universities, office buildings, municipal buildings, and housing. In 2000, Wolfdieter Dreibholz joined Coop Himmelb(l)au as CEO of Coop Himmelb(l)au Mex S.A. de C.V. and became a partner in Coop Himmelb(l)au Wolf D. Prix/ W. Dreibholz & Partner ZT GmbH, becoming CEO in 2004. Wolfdieter Dreibholz is a member of the chambers of architects of France, Austria and Italy and the author of numerous articles and research papers in the fields of architecture and urban planning.

Renowned and current projects

Coop Himmelb(l)au's best-known projects include: the Rooftop Re-modeling Falkestrasse in Vienna (1988); the "master plan" for the City of Melun-Sénart in France; the Groninger Museum, East Pavil-ion in Groningen (1994) in the Netherlands; the design for EXPO.02–Forum Arteplage in Biel, Switzerland; as well as the multifunctional UFA Cinema Center in Dresden, Germany (1998), the Academy of Fine Arts in Munich, Germany (2005) and the Akron Art Museum in Ohio, USA (2007). We have realized further key projects in Vienna in the past years, including the SEG Apartment Tower (1998), fol-lowed by the SEG Apartment Block Remise (2000); the Apartment Building Gasometer B (2001); and the Apartment and Office Build-ing, Schlachthausgasse (2005).

Among the recent projects that our studio is pursuing throughout the world is the BMW Welt in Munich, Germany, which will be opened on the 20th/21st of October 2007. Additionally, the Central Los Angeles Area High School #9 of Visual and Performing Arts in Los Angeles, is slated for 2008; the Musée des Confluences in Lyon, France for 2010; and the House of Music in Aalborg, Denmark for 2009.

In 2004, Coop Himmelb(l)au won first prize for the design of the build-ing for the European Central Bank's new headquarters in Frankfurt am Main, Germany, which is set for completion in 2011. In 2005, the jury for the competition to design the Busan Cinema Complex in Busan, South Korea (2010) again selected Coop Himmelb(l)au. And in 2006, our studio won first prize in a competition for the ex-pansion and new development of the Cloud Roof exhibition center in Riva del Garda, Italy (2009). For their design for the Museum of Contemporary Art & Planning Exhibition in Shenzhen, China, Coop Himmelb(l)au was nominated as winner of the competition in 2007.

Honors and awards

Over the course of the past three decades, Coop Himmelb(l)au has received numerous international awards. These include: the Förderungspreis für Baukunst, Berlin (1982), the Award of the City of Vienna for Architecture (1988), the Erich Schelling Architektur Preis (1992), the P. A. Award (1989, 1990, and 1991), the Grosser Österreichischer Staatspreis (1999) as well as the European Steel Design Award (2001). In December 2002, Coop Himmelb(l)au was made Officier de l'ordre des arts et des lettres and was awarded the Ehrenzeichen für Verdienste um das Land Wien. In 2005, for the design of the Akron Art Museum, our office received the American Architecture Award. Our office was awarded the 2007 International Architecture Award for four projects: for the Busan Cinema Com-plex, the Akademie der Bildenden Künste, the Great Egyptian Muse-um at the pyramids in Giza, and the Space of Contemporary Artistic Creation in Cordoba.

Exhibitions

Recognized as seminal for the architecture of the future, the works of Coop Himmelb(l)au have continually been the subject of interna-tional exhibitions. Among the largest and most widely known are the solo retrospectives Construire le Ciel in 1992 at the Centre Georges Pompidou in Paris, France, and the exhibition entitled Deconstruc-tivist Architecture held in 1988 at the Museum of Modern Art, New York, under the curatorship of Philip Johnson.

Internationally renowned institutions such as the Getty Foundation in Los Angeles, the Austrian Museum of Applied Arts/Contempo-rary Art (MAK) in Vienna and the Centre Georges Pompidou in Paris display the works of Coop Himmelb(l)au as part of their permanent exhibitions. In 1996, Coop Himmelb(l)au was invited to serve as the Austrian representative to the Sixth International Architecture Ex-hibition Biennale in Venice, Italy. Since then, our studio has been a regular participant, presenting several projects such as the Musée des Confluences and the Guangzhou Opera House. The Musée des Confluences in Lyon was additionally shown at the Latent Utopias exhibition in Graz, Austria, from October 2002 to March 2003.

Coop Himmelb(l)au has also been presented on several occasions at the Aedes East Gallery in Berlin, for example, at well-known shows such as Skyline in 1985, The Vienna Trilogy + One Cinema in 1998, and the exhibition on the competition for the BMW Event and Delivery Center in 2002. In the same year, Coop Himmelb(l)au was also present at the International Architecture Exhibition Biennale in Venice, Italy with the projects BMW Welt and a design for the new World Trade Center. In December 2007, our studio will be featured in the exhibition Beyond the Blue at the MAK in Vienna.

Last but not least, Coop Himmelb(l)au has also designed several exhibitions. Among our best known works are Paradise Cage: Kiki Smith and Coop Himmelb(l)au, shown in 1996 at the Museum of Contemporary Art in Los Angeles, and in 2000 Rudi Gernreich: Fashion will go out of fashion, for the Steirischer Herbst festival in Graz, Austria, which also traveled to Philadelphia, USA.

Projects (Selection)

Museum of Contemporary Art & Planning Exhibition, Shenzhen, China (2007–)

Sea-Life Centre, Vienna, Austria (2006–)

Cloud Roof, Riva del Garda, Italy (2006–)

Busan Cinema Complex, Pusan International Film Festival, Busan, South Korea (2006–)

European Central Bank (ECB), Frankfurt, Germany (2003–)

Central Los Angeles Area High School #9 for Visual and Performing Arts, Los Angeles, USA (2002–)

House of Music, Aalborg, Denmark (2002–)

Villa Soravia, Millstatt, Austria (2001–2006)

Hammerhead Communities, Outer Banks, North Carolina, USA (2001–)

BMW Welt, Munich, Germany (2001–2007)

Musée des Confluences, Lyon, France (2001–)

Akron Art Museum, Ohio, USA (2001–2007)

Apartment and Office Building Schlachthausgasse, Vienna, Austria (2001/2003–2005)

Fashion will go out of Fashion, Rudi Gernreich (Exhibition), Graz, Austria (2000)

Apartment Building "Liesing Brewery" Vienna, Austria (2002/2006–)

Town Town — Office Tower, Vienna, Austria (2000/2005–)

Apartment Towers "Wienerberg City", Vienna, Austria (1999–2004)

Expo.02 — Forum Arteplage Biel, Switzerland (1999–2002)

Exhibitioncenter Hainburg (Competition, 1st prize), Austria (1999)

Restaurant Mosku, Guadalajara, Mexico (1999/2008–)

Ödipus Rex (Stage design), Amsterdam, Netherlands (1998)

Otis College of Art and Design (Competition), Los Angeles, USA (1998)

JVC New Urban Entertainment Center, Guadalajara, Mexico (1998/2008–)

Paradise Cage (Exhibition design), MOCA, Los Angeles, USA (1996)

Apartment Building Gasometer B, Vienna, Austria (1995–2001)

The Media Pavilion (Exhibition), Biennale di Venezia, Italy (1995)

Cloud #9 (Competition), Uno Geneva, Switzerland (1995)

SEG Apartment Block Remise, Vienna, Austria (1994–2000)

SEG Apartment Tower, Vienna, Austria (1994–1998)

Expressionist Utopias (Exhibition design), LACMA, Los Angeles, USA (1993)

Der Weltbaumeister (Stage design), Graz, Austria (1993)

UFA Cinema Center, Dresden, Germany (1993–1998)

Office and Research Center Seibersdorf, Austria (1991–1995)

Groninger Museum, The East Pavilion, Groningen, Netherlands (1993–1994)

Apartment Building Tautenhayngasse, Vienna, Austria (1992/2000–2002)

Academy of Fine Arts, Munich, Germany (1992/2002–2005)

Contruire Le Ciel, Centre Pompidou (Exhibition), Paris, France (1992–1993)

German Museum of Hygiene (Competition, 1st prize), Dresden, Germany (1992)

Guggenheim Museum (Competition), Bilbao, Spain (1991)

Rehak House, Los Angeles, USA (1990/1991–1992)

Funder Factory, St. Veit/Glan, Austria (1988–1989)

The Heart of a City, Melun-Sénart (Competition, 1st prize), Paris, France (1986–1987)

Studio Baumann, Vienna, Austria (1984–1985)

Rooftop Remodelling Falkestraße, Vienna, Austria (1983–1988)

Open House, Malibu, California, USA (1983/1988–1989)

The Red Angel, Vienna, Austria (1980–1981)

Reiss Bar, Vienna, Austria (1977)

WITH GENEROUS SUPPORT FROM

ArcelorMittal Building & Construction Support
Germany, Austria, Switzerland
Subbelrather Strasse 13, 50672 Cologne, Germany

bfm – Büro für Messeplanung
Forstenrieder Allee 139, 81476 Munich, Germany

B + G Ingenieure Bollinger und Grohmann GmbH
Westhafenplatz 1, 60327 Frankfurt/Main, Germany

Bosch Sicherheitssysteme GmbH Niederlassung Munich
Robert-Koch-Strasse 100, 85521 Ottobrunn, Germany

Casalis
Wielsbeeksestrasse 8, 8710 Ooipem, Belgium

Fuhrmann Visuelle Leitsysteme
Eichenweg 1, 96215 Lichtenfels, Germany

Josef Gartner GmbH
Gartnerstrasse 20, 89423 Gundelfingen, Germany

Kühn Bauer & Partner Beratende Ingenieure GmbH
Wilhelm-Wagenfald-Strasse 6, 80807 Munich, Germany

Lummel GmbH & Co. KG
Bedachungen und Fassaden in Metall
Echterstrasse 65, 97753 Karlstadt/Main, Germany

mg ingenieure management · consulting
Elisabeth-Christinen-Strasse 4, 13156 Berlin, Germany

Peters · Schüßler · Sperr
Ingenieurbüro für Bauwesen GmbH
Bucher Strasse 3, 90419 Nuremberg, Germany

Hubert Pupeter GmbH
Estrichbau
Hans-Böckler-Strasse 4, 86551 Aichach, Germany

Ingenieurbüro Pro-Elektroplan
Otto-Hahn-Strasse 40, 85521 Ottobrunn/Munich, Germany

pbb Elisabeth Balke Architekten Innenarchitekten
Friedrich-Herschel-Strasse 1, 81679 Munich, Germany

R B S Projektmanagement GmbH Unternehmensberatung
Knorrstrasse 142/V, 80937 Munich, Germany

Fliesen Röhlich GmbH
Zum Handwerkerhof 9, 90530 Wendelstein, Germany

Ingenieurbüro Schönenberg + Partner
Rüdesheimer Strasse 15, 80686 Munich, Germany

Schmidt Stumpf Frühauf und Partner Ingenieurgesellschaft m.b.H.
Leopoldstrasse 208, 80804 Munich, Germany

Solarstromanlagen-Spezialist
SunStrom GmbH
Moritzburger Weg 67, 01109 Dresden, Germany

theater projekte daberto + kollegen planungsgesellschaft mbh
Augustenstrasse 59, 80333 Munich, Germany

Vitra GmbH
Charles-Eames-Straße 2, 79576 Weil am Rhein, Germany

Vollet Anlagenbau GmbH + Co. KG
Stadtseestrasse 12, 74189 Weinsberg, Germany

Waagner-Biro Austria Stage Systems AG
Stadlauerstrasse 54, 1221 Vienna, Austria

PUBLISHER'S INFORMATION

Technical Description Paul Kath
with the help of: Klaus Bollinger, Manfred Grohmann, Jörg Schneider and Daniel Pfanner (Double Cone, Roof and Facade); Michael Kühn and Bernd Ropeter jun. (Technology, Construction and Energy Design); Reinhold Daberto (Forum); Wilfried Kramb (Daylight and Artificial Light); Siegfried Baumgartner and Stefan Holst (Solar Power System); Hans Lechner and Sabine Liebenau (Project Structure); Ferdinand Tremmel (Lounge); Rüdiger Schidzig, Stefan Wagner, Dr. Johann Köppl, Josef Ludwig, Jochen Peters, Harald Pässler (ARGE Tragwerksplanung BMW Welt: Double Cone, Roof and Facade / Construction Execution)

Photo credits The publishers have made every effort to credit all copyright holders. Any rights owner who has been omitted is asked to please notify the publisher so that this can be corrected.

Front section
Hélène Binet: photos 4, 5, 6, 7, 10, 11
Ari Marcopoulos: photos 2, 3, 8, 9
Gerald Zugmann: photo 1
Back section
Hélène Binet: photos 9, 10, 12
Ari Marcopoulos: photos 1, 2, 5, 6
Gerald Zugmann: photos 3, 4, 7, 8, 11

© COOP HIMMELB(L)AU: all photographs, plans and texts, if not otherwise indicated. Hélène Binet: Cover, pp. 23, 173, 216–217; Marcus Buck: pp. 14 below, 25, 79, 82–83, 85, 89, 91, 94–95, 97, 99, 117, 122–123, 126–127, 130–131, 139, 142–143, 145, 159, 161, 168–169, 176–177, 184–185, 189, 199, 200, 203, 211, 213, 219, 226–227, 237; Armin Hess, ISOCHROM: pp. 32, 33, 34, 35, 36, 106 above, 120–121; Paul Kath: pp. 156–157, 181, 193; Ari Marcopoulos: pp. 93, 100, 101, 102–103, 118, 119, 148–149, 152–153, 164–165, 175, 179, 182, 183, 194–195, 206–207, 222–223, 233, 234, 238–239; Iwan Baan: pp. 150, 151, 163; Volker Moehrke p. 29; Aleksandra Pawloff: p. 2; Markus Pillhofer: pp. 30, 33 above, 109 left; Ferdinand Tremmel: pp. 70–71; Gert Winkler: p. 12 above; Gertrud Wolfschwenger: p. 9; Gerald Zugmann: pp. 12 below, 19; US Air Force: p. 8; Interfoto/picturedesk.com: p. 10; Geoff Winningham: p. 14 above; Reiner Zettl: p. 17 below.

Editor Kristin Feireiss
Project Management for Publisher Anja Besserer

Book Project Team at COOP HIMMELB(L)AU Wolf D. Prix, Cynthia Kallmeyer, Paul Kath, Timo Rieke, Anja Sorger, Emilia Margaretha, Isabelle Ost, Caroline Ecker, Angelika Pöschl, Martina Wallner

German texts translated into English by Jennifer Taylor-Gaida and Michael Scuffil for alpha & bet VERLAGSSERVICE, Munich
Copyedited by John Sykes, Cologne and Dr. Willfried Baatz, alpha & bet VERLAGSSERVICE, Munich
Design and Typesetting Sophie Bleifuß with Michael Uszinski, Berlin
Production Siegmar Hiller, HillerMedien, Berlin
Origination Bildpunkt, Berlin
Printing and Binding Druckerei Uhl, Radolfzell

COOP HIMMELB(L)AU
Wolf D. Prix / W. Dreibholz & Partner ZT GmbH
Spengergasse 37
1050 Vienna
Tel. +49 (0)1 546 60
Fax +49 (0)1 546 60 600
www.coop-himmelblau.at

Library of Congress Control Number 2007936415

A catalogue record for this book is available from the British Library; Deutsche Nationalbibliothek holds a record of this publication in the Deutsche Nationalbibliografie; detailed bibliographical data can be found under: http://dnb.ddb.de

© Prestel Verlag, Munich · Berlin · London · New York, 2007

Printed in Germany on acid-free paper.

Prestel Verlag
Königinstrasse 9
80539 Munich
Tel. +49 (0)89 24 29 08-300
Fax +49 (0)89 24 29 08-335
www.prestel.de

Prestel Publishing Ltd.
4 Bloomsbury Place
London WC1A 2QA
Tel. +44 (0)20 7323-5004
Fax +44 (0)20 7636-8004

Prestel Publishing
900 Broadway, Suite 603
New York, NY 10003
Tel. +1 (212) 995 2720
Fax +1 (212) 995 2733
www.prestel.com

ISBN 978-3-7913-3876-7 (English trade edition)
ISBN 978-3-7913-3875-0 (German trade edition)

fabulous

FIFTIES

Designs for Modern Living

Pink and black ducks, and a bowl marked "Stanford,
S., Ohio" on the bottom. Bowl: 13.5" wide. Ducks:
8.5" high.